Being An Aries

Aries

All Day, Every Day
An Autobiographical Guide 2020

By M. C. Williams

@www.copyright.gov

Table of Contents

Prologue……………….….page 5

The Basics……………..….page 9

The Break Down……….page 11

Aries Children…………. page 20

Aries Teenagers……….page 36

Aries Women………….page 39

Aries Men………....…..page 44

Aries Parents………….page 46

Aries Relationships…..page 50

Aries Friends..………..page 60

Aries Negative Energy...page 64

Aries Gifts…............…..page 68

Things We Need To Work On
…...........................…..….page 71

Interactions with Other Signs

    Aries…..........…page 73

    Taurus….....…page 90

    Gemini…........…page 100

    Cancer….....…page 110

    Leo….........….page 120

    Virgo…....…...page 131

    Libra….......….page 136

Scorpio..........page 146

Sagittarius........page 160

Capricorn........page 169

Aquarius.........page 177

Pisces.............page 182

Prologue

I am an Aries. My father was an Aries. I have Aries friends and I work with Aries people every day. After I sat and thought about writing this book, I realized that some of what I know may be useful to others and that I have a large volume of experiences to share based on astrological signs. I make it my mission to find out the signs of the people I am around. It helps me when I have to interact with them.

You may not be an Aries, but I bet you know a few. You may be dating one, married to one, have a parent who is one, have Aries children or best friends. You may secretly admire them and hate them at the same time. We know.

This book is based on my experiences as an Aries. My reaction to the things I have witnessed other signs do and how I view their behavior. I became interested in astrology when I was ten or so. I did my research and I observe people. In my forty-nine years on this planet, I have noticed similarities in signs and how they interact with me as an Aries.

This is not a scientific astrological study. It is not based on the moon or any birth chart although, I will reference my birth chart from time to time. This book is to help anyone who wants to know how to understand and to see how an Aries thinks and behaves. If you are an Aries, you will find that some of the things done in this book have been done by you as well. I find the situations that have occurred are amusing as I look back on them but, not amusing as I was going through it.

There are a lot of rumors and false information about us. If you want to know us, ask us. When I was growing up, I always heard bad things about my sign and people would say, "that's how you are." I wanted to disagree, but I would only shrug my shoulders. I'm not going to argue with anyone about who I am. If that's what you want to believe, fine. You don't know me. Everything I do, I have a reason for doing it. I see the outcomes before they happen, and I plan accordingly.

Aries are complicated, so if you are trying to marry one of us, this will help. If you just want to get along with us, you really need to understand a few things. Aries get along with all signs if we have to work with you, but we require honesty. If you are our friends, you will think we are picking on you or bullying you, but we are trying to get to the bottom of the situation. We get frustrated when we don't know something, and you will think we are mad at you. We are not. We will tell you if we are angry with you. You would know an angry Aries if you saw one.

Aries come across as blunt, rude and aggressive. There are Aries who are quiet, who don't want conflict, and who will work hard at getting along. Some of us are a mixture of both. You should find out the other planets that influence you by doing a birth chart. The way I get along with Tauruses and Scorpios will not be the same for you because my birth chart has a lot of planets in Earth signs and Water signs. This makes my relationships with them easier than Aries who don't have these planets in their birth chart. You can get your chart by going to astrotheme.com or astrology.com. You can get a free birth chart from a lot of sites if you google "astrology birth chart." For your birth chart to be accurate, you will need to know your time of birth.

I am including my birth chart as a reference and it may inspire you to discover yours:

Sun sign: Aries
Moon sign: Gemini
Mercury: Taurus
Venus: Taurus
Mars: Taurus
Jupiter: Scorpio
Saturn: Taurus
Uranus: Libra
Neptune: Sagittarius
Pluto: Pisces
Rising sign: Scorpio

This book is going to give you examples of things we do, things we like, and things we don't like as an Aries. Hopefully, it will help you understand your Aries friends and even yourself. This book is not fiction because everything that I mention in this book happened and is based on my experiences.

*Disclaimer: My views don't represent the views of all Aries. You may not get my sense of humor. You may find this information to be useless. Everything in this book is true and factual. The entertainment value is priceless.

The Basics

Sign	Birth Range
Aries	March 21 – April 19
Taurus	April 20 – May 20
Gemini	May 21 – June 20
Cancer	June 21 – July 22
Leo	July 23 – August 22
Virgo	August 23 – September 22
Libra	September 23 – October 22
Scorpio	October 23 – November 21
Sagittarius	November 22 – December 21
Capricorn	December 22 – January 19
Aquarius	January 20 – February 18
Pisces	February 19 – March 20

Sign	Symbol	Keyword
Aries	Ram	I am
Taurus	Bull	I have
Gemini	Twins	I think
Cancer	Crab	I feel
Leo	Lion	I will
Virgo	Virgin	I analyze
Libra	Scales	I balance
Scorpio	Scorpion	I desire
Sagittarius	Archer/Centaur	I

		understand
Capricorn	Goat	I use
Aquarius	Water Bearer	I know
Pisces	Fishes	I believe

Sign	Element	Quality
Aries	Fire	Cardinal
Taurus	Earth	Fixed
Gemini	Air	Mutable
Cancer	Water	Cardinal
Leo	Fire	Fixed
Virgo	Earth	Mutable
Libra	Air	Cardinal
Scorpio	Water	Fixed
Sagittarius	Fire	Mutable
Capricorn	Earth	Cardinal
Aquarius	Air	Fixed
Pisces	Water	Mutable

The Break Down

How Other Signs Feel About Aries

Aries – Finally, someone who is just like me. We will have fun together.

Taurus – Aries seems to have their lives together. I will ask for advice.

Gemini – Aries gets my sense of humor. They act like me.

Cancer – Aries makes me forget about being sad. I wish they thought about me more.

Leo – I love how you praise me. Aries makes me want to show off.

Virgo – Aries appreciates my attention to detail. I wish I could let things slide like an Aries.

Libra – I like how Aries looks at me. Aries lets me be myself.

Scorpio – Aries honesty makes me want to marry them. I wish I could control them.

Sagittarius – Aries listens to me philosophize. I can teach Aries what I know.

Capricorn –Arguing with an Aries is foreplay. They are useful.

Aquarius – We have so much fun together. Hanging out with an Aries is easy.

Pisces –Aries is the only person who helps me. I can say strange things to an Aries and not feel weird.

What Irritates Aries About Other Signs

Aries – We are too similar. We like it at first, then we don't. They challenge everything we say, and we challenge them. They want to do things and so do we. We argue about which things to do. Which one of us is the most important in this relationship? We will have to share the spotlight.

Taurus – They move too slow. Everything takes extra time. They are always calm in the face of adversity. This can calm us or piss us off. They think we are ridiculous for getting angry so fast. Things that make us angry don't bother them.

Gemini – They change their minds too much. We don't know what they are talking about from minute to minute. They are never around when you need them. They are always out and about. When you want to stay home and spend time with them, they will invite friends over.

Cancer – They are overly sensitive. It's okay to be upset but not every day. Everything brings on an emotional response. Everything an Aries does is questioned. They think we are doing things to hurt them on purpose. They want us to consider them in everything we do. This is annoying.

Leo – They brag a lot. Leos are great, we know. They like attention. They like to get compliments. We don't mind their behavior unless it is extreme. Some of them are too extreme. Too loud and too extravagant and it annoys us when we want to go under the radar. They can never go under the radar. They bring a lot of attention to themselves.

Virgo – They can't let go of small problems. We don't want to hear them complain about a hangnail. They want things to be perfect. They can't make any moves until things are the way they want them. They don't seem happy unless they are in someone's business. They try to give Aries advice we didn't ask for. The downfall of others makes them happy.

Libra – They are too indecisive. They never know what they want to eat or see or do. When they make a decision, wait a minute, they change their minds often. They don't know when they are happy or what makes them happy. We think they are happy, and they will say they are not. They smile at things that should not make them smile. They frown at things that make other people happy. They are off balance.

Scorpio – They are too mysterious to the point of being downright deceitful. If you ask them what they are doing, the answer is vague. They will manipulate you to their will. They will sulk if they don't get what they want. Their mood changes often. They tend to be negative. They have an addictive spirit which means they tend to overdo it with drugs, alcohol, and sex.

Sagittarius – They say they want to do things, but you never see them doing those things. They are content with basic needs. They are not impressed with fame or fortune. They will tell you about things you are not interested in knowing. They behave like senseis, philosophers or professors no matter what type of job they have. They would rather read than work.

Capricorn – They don't give us enough attention. Capricorns have a tendency to focus on work and it takes over their lives. They like to argue. Aries won't back down, but we would rather not argue. They have a negative view of the world. Aries would rather see things in a positive light.

Aquarius – They are too independent. We want to spend time with them, but they want to be alone. They have a lot of friends and we don't like all of their friends. They talk a lot which we like but it is mostly gossip which we don't like. We listen because it is interesting, but we have no gossip to add to the conversation.

Pisces – Their behavior is unpredictable. One minute happy, next minute angry. They entertain us with their jokes about people. They see things on another level, and this amuses an Aries. Pisces believe things that are not true.

What other signs don't like about Aries

Aries – The arguments. Aries don't back down from an argument. That is the problem. We are you and you are us. Someone will have to be the loser. Aries hate to lose. Aries makes them angry.

Taurus – An Aries will interrupt them when they are talking. Aries wants to ask questions. Aries wants them to get to the point, and we make the Taurus forget what they were about to say. Aries gets angry too quickly about things Taurus finds unimportant. Aries makes them angry.

Gemini – An Aries will stop listening to them. Aries don't want to hang out all the time. Aries will get missing and Gemini will have to find someone else to hang with. Aries has too many other things to do. Aries makes them angry.

Cancer – An Aries will not take Cancer's emotions seriously because they are emotional too frequently. Cancers believe Aries are inconsiderate because we don't include them when we make decisions. Aries makes them angry.

Leo – An Aries will forget about them and will do other things without them. Aries doesn't spend enough time with them. Aries will not agree with all of their silly schemes. Aries will tell them they are getting on their nerves. Aries doesn't need them. Aries is as successful as a Leo. Aries makes them angry.

Virgo – Aries is too confident. Virgos can't understand where our confidence comes from since we are far from perfect. Aries never pay attention to detail. Aries wings everything (it's not true but that is what they think). Aries is not afraid. Aries makes them angry.

Libra –Aries kindness makes them jealous. Aries are natural givers and Libras give out of obligation. Aries do things because they want to, and Libras feel like they have to do things to make people happy. Aries knows when Libras are lying. Aries will argue with them and win. Aries makes them angry.

Scorpio –Aries can't be manipulated. Aries draws them out of their shell. Aries wants to know their secrets. Aries is moody. Aries can match their intensity. Aries know too much about them. Aries makes them angry.

Sagittarius – Aries will interrupt them in the middle of their conversation. Aries calls them on their bullshit. Aries will correct them when they are wrong. Aries will change the subject for no reason. Aries will walk away from a conversation. Aries makes them angry.

Capricorn – Aries are too aggressive. Aries are competitive. Aries will try new things. Aries seems immature. Aries wants to have fun. Aries wants too much attention. Aries makes them angry.

Aquarius – Aries can move on from a relationship too fast. Aries makes mistakes but doesn't stop living. Aries will take a risk. Something is always happening to an Aries. Aries gets more attention than them. Aries makes them angry.

Pisces – Aries has a positive outlook. Aries can always find a bright side. Aries makes them forget how bad things are and will change their mood. Aries laugh at their drama. Aries makes them angry.

How Aries feel about other signs

Aries – Aries like the passion and the adventure of another Aries. Aries don't care what you do as long as you don't interfere with what I am doing.

Taurus – Aries likes that they don't judge us. Aries don't care what you do as long as you don't interfere with what I am doing.

Gemini – Aries likes their style and they throw fabulous parties. Aries don't care what you do as long as you don't interfere with what I am doing.

Cancer – Cancers wants our opinion and emotional support. Aries don't care what you do as long as you don't interfere with what I am doing.

Leo – Aries see Leos as exciting and positive. Aries don't care what you do as long as you don't interfere with what I am doing.

Virgo – Aries feels that Virgos are good at plotting and planning. Aries don't care what you do as long as you don't interfere with what I am doing.

Libra – Aries finds Libras to be very attractive. Aries don't care what you do as long as you don't interfere with what I am doing.

Scorpio – Aries likes the mystery and intensity. Aries don't care what you do as long as you don't interfere with what I am doing.

Sagittarius – Aries likes the conversation. Aries don't care what you do as long as you don't interfere with what I am doing.

Capricorn – Aries likes their stability and work ethic. Aries don't care what you do as long as you don't interfere with what I am doing.

Aquarius – They are always doing something unusual. Aries don't care what you do as long as you don't interfere with what I am doing.

Pisces – Their opinions about other people are usually correct and they have our back. Aries don't care what you do as long as you don't interfere with what I am doing.

Aries Children

Aries children are adventurous. They want to see and touch everything. Aries children are listening and watching everyone. They will imitate you and do what you do and say.

You think they are busy doing something, but they are also, paying attention to you. We multitask at an early age. One Aries child will keep you busy. If you plan to have a large family, you may want to space when you have an Aries child with other children. You will be overwhelmed if you have an Aries and other child around the same age. The Aries child will get into things while you are not looking. The Aries child will keep you running around and removing harmful things out of their way.

Aries children are always getting injured. Make sure your home is child proof because we tend to amass battle scars. We play a little rougher than the other kids because we like to have fun. I was always getting hurt from bike riding, running, climbing trees, or trying something dangerous. I wasn't afraid of anything. I remember always being rushed to the emergency room or having to get bruises patched up. I blacked out once from falling out of a tree.

Aries children need to be watched or else they will get into things. As a child, I burned my hand trying to imitate my mother ironing clothes. I burned my leg trying to pour myself hot water to make tea. I remember things clearly from before I was five years old. I wasn't yet in kindergarten because I was at home with my parents and siblings.

Aries children often learn to speak quickly. If you read books to them, they will memorize what you are reading. Aries children like to learn and play. The more things you have for them to do the better. There should be a lot of activities for Aries children. Aries children are content playing by themselves. They get along with other children, but they are watchful of other children. They will imitate other children's behaviors as well. If a kid eats a crayon, the Aries child will try it. If another child hits the Aries child, they will hit the other child back.

Trying to punish the Aries child is not the answer. Talk to the child, reprimand them by saying no. Aries children don't require a lot of punishment in the beginning stages. Firm words and repeated actions work best.

Your Aries child will seem pretty smart. That's because he or she is paying attention and have a great memory. They will do things that will amaze you. Those things are things they saw someone else do. They have excellent memories. The best thing to do with such an active mind is to teach it.

Teach your child words, spelling, and the alphabet at an early age. It is never too early. Don't be afraid or intimidated by it. Eventually, this will slow down as soon as they get around other kids and pick up undesirable habits. While you have their full attention, use it to give them the foundation of learning.

If you want to know how smart your Aries child is at four, ask him or her a serious question. Like, why do you think daddy has to go to work every day or do you think you should work when you grow up? You might be surprised.

My mother read nursery rhymes to me as a toddler. I memorized them. A relative came to the house when I was "reading" a book that my mother had read to me numerous times before. I was two years old. Needless to say, my relative thought I was a child genius. I had learned to memorize the book and eventually, was able to recognize the words as words. Elementary school was easy for me.

The best thing my mother did for me was read books to me and my brothers. That was where my love for words began. I stayed in the library. I read books an eight-year-old probably shouldn't have read. I loved when we had book fairs at school. I got a lot of books. I loved it so much that I started creating poems at six and then wrote my first book at eight.

If your Aries child has a talent, let him or her explore it. Buy books, let them join clubs and sports. The more they have to do the better. For example, one of the guys I was friends with didn't have any extracurricular activities in school. I hung out with him until I started playing sports. This guy who was an Aries started taking drugs in elementary school because he was imitating his older brother.

Another Aries guy I went to school with got into a lot of trouble fighting. By the time we were teenagers, one had a drug problem and the other one was becoming a delinquent. We have to direct our energy in good channels, or we lose control and make bad decisions. As the parent of Aries children, it would be wise to keep your kids in some activity other than school. My son is a Leo, but he is an Aries rising. He was a very active little boy. I made sure to put him in sports even though he wasn't interested at all. He turned out to be very good at basketball.

What is an Aries rising? Your rising sign is the sign you were born under based on your time of birth. I was born April tenth at 7:49 pm which makes my rising sign Scorpio. My son was born August thirteenth, his time of birth was 22:21pm which makes him an Aries rising. If you want to learn more about your birth chart you can go to astrotheme.com or astrology.com to find out what other signs are in your birth chart.

The rising sign or Ascendant is the sign that influences how people see you or how you react in situations. It is important to know what your rising sign is because it will explain why people see you the way they do. I could never understand why people said I was sneaky. I am not sneaky but that is how I appear because I can go from outspoken (Aries) to quiet or withdrawn (Scorpio). I will withhold information and keep other people's secrets. These are things Scorpios are accustomed to doing. When in a crowd, I am the one slinking around in the dark (Scorpio) until someone notices me and then, I am the life of the party (Aries). I have a lot of confidence (Aries) but I like to talk about deep topics (Scorpio).

As a Leo, my son didn't care a bit about school, but he was smart as a whip (Aries). He was always getting into things (Aries) and is the kid everyone wants to be around (Leo). Like me, he needs his down time to get his energy up.

I was an excellent reader at five. I know because I read the curse words written on the bathroom walls and on the poles in the school yard. I sounded them out and would ask my mother what they meant when I went home. I knew what they meant.

Before my mother had other children, I had all the attention I needed as a child from my grandparents. Probably too much attention as I would imitate them. I was "grown." When my siblings came along, I wanted to help. In my head, I was a little adult. I would try to pick up my baby brother and feed him all because I saw other people doing it. Aries children see everything. Even things you may not want them to see.

I was a fairly talkative kid. I wouldn't let anyone push me around. If someone hit me, I hit them back. If someone said something to me that I didn't like, I had a response. I was never the quiet and afraid type. I played rough and I would fight but only if someone else started it. It never occurred to me not to like someone so when kids didn't like me, I was confused. As an adult, I realize that I am annoying because I want to know everything. I am a pest when I am curious. I won't stop until I get answers.

My grandmother is a Leo and my mother is a Libra. When I was three, we went to visit some relatives who lived in New Jersey. I was happy about it because I like all of my relatives and I had never met these kids. I tried to play nice with this one girl who was older than me, but she was not having it. She gave me her toy but then, she grabbed her toy from me and hit me. I was in shock because I was not expecting that. I grabbed the toy from her and slapped her to the floor. My grandmother saw the whole incident and I was scared I was going to get in trouble because I didn't want to hit the girl in her own home, but she shouldn't have hit me first. I looked over at my grandmother and she was smiling. The cousin is crying because she was shocked. Apparently, she was considered to be tough. My mother comes over and spanks me, but my grandmother was angry which confused my mother.

My grandmother said, "that girl hit Melony first and she deserved what she got." Let me tell you, I always loved my grandmother but for her to defend me against my mother who in my opinion had no idea how to raise me, made me love my grandmother more (if that was possible). I would have benefited from a parent who asked me what happened or who had a bit more understanding. I was fortunate to have my grandmother who didn't see my behavior as bad. The last thing you need to do is label your Aries child as "bad." We are defenders and peacemakers. Most of us are not going around picking fights or starting trouble but we are not backing away from a challenge.

Aries children are born with self-confidence. This is a good thing. You don't have to try to make them have less of it, the world will do that, and they will learn to manage it. Aries children need to have a place where they feel safe and can come home to talk about what they learned in school and to brag a little. Aries children like to be the smartest and the kindest.

We are usually the teacher's helper until the other kids give us a hard time about it. We make friends easily. We are popular because we are smart and kind. We will share our lunch. We will sit with the kid who is sitting by himself. We will help the kid who doesn't know what page the class assignment is on. We will defend our friends in a fight.

We are protective of our siblings and relatives. When I was seven, I had cousins from Mississippi come to visit. They were poor and my father paid for them to come visit us in New York. It was three girls and their grandmother who was our aunt. We spent all our time outside back then running and playing. We were running and one of the cousins tripped and all I could think about was I was going to get into trouble because I was the oldest and they were poor. So, I jumped in front of her and she fell on me. She bruised her arm but nothing more. I, on the other hand, had to go to the emergency room. I scraped a plug the size of a quarter out of my hair and banged myself up pretty bad. Of course, I got scolded and no one asked me what happened. Back then, parents didn't ask any questions. I still get frustrated when I think about how many times things could have been better if someone had just asked me what happened. I know for myself that I made the best decision. I cost my dad probably twenty dollars to patch me up whereas taking my cousin to the hospital for the same injuries would have cost him thousands out of pocket. That is how far ahead I was thinking at seven.

Aries children rarely start out afraid and withdrawn. We can be quiet when we are learning something new, but we want to answer all the questions. We don't like to be ignored if we know the answer. We like to read out loud and we like doing homework.

Aries children who have not been given the best upbringing or who are not confident, will tend to be withdrawn and quiet. You may not know the difference because Aries children who have a great upbringing have their moments of quiet withdrawal. The difference is that when an Aries doesn't get the benefit of a good upbringing, they will either not defend themselves or over defend themselves.

Aries children's minds develop early. I remember thinking critically and making plans at five. For example, I walked to school in the morning when I was five with other kids in the neighborhood. We walked six blocks, but it was okay because there were other kids walking. One day, the school decided that some kids had to go home for lunch and then come back to school. Lunch was only forty-five minutes. I knew it would take me more than forty-five minutes to walk home, eat lunch and then walk back to school. So, when the teacher said, I was one of the kids who had to go home for lunch I knew I wasn't going to walk back. Not only that, I lived the furthest.

Why my mother didn't know this is beyond me. I walked all the way home and she asked me what I was doing there. I told her we had a half day at school. I was prepared to tell her that kindergarten was going to be a half a day until school ended if that is what it took for me to not have to walk back to school after lunch. She didn't call the school and she didn't question me any further. Besides, I was five. What did I know?

When school was over, my teacher Mrs. Bang, came to the house. I was surprised. I didn't think she would miss me with a classroom full of kids. I stood in the doorway while she was talking to my mother who had no idea that I was going to have to walk home for lunch every day. I was thinking as they were talking that I was not going to do it anyway, so my school days would end at 12 noon.

My absence really scared the daylights out of my young white teacher who thought I might have gotten kidnapped. She and I both knew I shouldn't be walking home from school by myself regardless of the school policy or my mother's oblivious attitude. I have to say, I used to wonder about my mother during times like these. She never said what I expected a mother to say.

The next day, my teacher had me sit next to her during lunch and eventually, the school policy was changed. I didn't care either way because if they sent me home, I would not return to school. I had made up my mind about it already. I was a little disappointed that I had to spend the full day in school, but I got over it.

I loved learning. Anything my teachers taught me, I learned fast. I loved school. I knew everyone and everyone knew me. I had a best friend because I gave her a nickel for lunch when she didn't have any lunch money. We were friends until we graduated from high school. She is a Taurus.

My Taurus friend and I were very different, but it worked for us. I was a tom boy and she was not. She was quiet in school and I liked to raise my hand and answer questions.

Boys liked her but she didn't give them the time of day. Most of my friends were boys. The boys I was friends with were Aries. We climbed trees, we rode bikes, and we wrestled. They hung out with me and my Capricorn brother and my Sagittarius brother, who were both younger than me. My Pisces brother was too young to play with us. Most of the time, he would watch us play or go stay in the house.

Our shenanigans began in the first grade. I enjoyed being free. I came home and did my homework and then headed out to play. Most Aries kids like to spend time outside. Back then, everyone played outside. If we don't go outside, we will play rough in the house. Aries kids have to have a lot of things to do to keep them active. A bored Aries will be grumpy and argumentative.

Aries children will challenge their siblings. We want them to know who is in charge. When I was about ten, a girl moved into the neighborhood who was an Aries. She had two older brothers. One of her brothers is a Pisces and the other is an Aries and her mother is a Sagittarius. Even when I was young, I was fascinated with astrology. People are more similar than you can imagine.

This girl and I became fast friends, but like my Taurus friend, she was more of a girly-girl. What was similar about us is that we liked adventure whereas my Taurus friend didn't come out much. Soon I was balancing my hanging out with the guys with hanging out with the girls. I hung out with the Taurus at school but walked to school with the Aries. I hung out with the boys after school because the Aries friend couldn't come out to play. I was able to visit some of my other friends when the kids in the neighborhood weren't available.

I was one of those kids that didn't stay home much. Part of that was because I couldn't get any peace and quiet at my house. Even though Aries like to play and be active, we need quiet time to refuel. I didn't like when I couldn't get any peace because it made me very argumentative. To this day, I don't like being tired.

Aries tend to get up at the last minute and have to rush to get to school on time. My Aries friend and I were always late and had to run to get to school before the bell rang.

In the first grade, our school started having activities that kids could join. I had no interest in joining anything. My life was pretty full as far as I was concerned. My Taurus friend asked me to join a lot of after school groups with her, stuff she liked. I didn't care. If it wasn't for her, I wouldn't have joined band and played the flute, I wouldn't have joined gymnastics or basketball or the chorus. If she wanted me to join, I did. I found out I was good at doing stuff other than climbing trees and popping wheelies on my bike. I stayed in all of these activities because she was in them. If it was up to me, I would have quit.

I learned some other things about myself in first grade as well. I was having a really bad day and as I sat in the auditorium with the whole school, I was feeling overwhelmed. This would be the first time and the last time I cried in public. I can't remember why I felt so overwhelmed, but I remember thinking I am on my own. My brothers are younger than me and won't be able to defend me. I will have to take care of myself. One kid noticed me silently sobbing and asked me if I was ok. I nodded yes, but I wasn't. I had the weight of the world on my shoulders. I had to figure out how to take care of myself and my little brothers against the world. Although, that was a sad day for me, it was the day I because unstoppable. If I had to fight people, I would. I didn't care how big they were or if they had older brothers and sisters. After I consoled myself, whatever it was I was worried about or afraid of disappeared.

The one thing I wish I had was an older sibling to talk to, but I wasn't blessed with that. When I think of it now, how my friends who had older brothers and sisters were tortured by them, I was lucky. I was the oldest and no one told me what to do. The thing I enjoyed most about childhood was the freedom and the learning.

Aries Teenager

The hardest part of my life was my teenage years. I discovered boys. As a tomboy, I had a lot of male friends, but I wasn't interested in any of them. I wanted to know how to kiss and I would do that but that was as far as I was interested. The misconception was that because I was "nice," I would fall in love. I was not in love with anyone. I was infatuated. I didn't want to hurt anyone's feelings but nevertheless, feelings got hurt.

When puberty hit, the boys lost their minds trying to have sex. I found out that a lot of the girls I thought were my friends weren't.

Some were jealous of my friendship with the guys because they were interested in them. I was a bit weird because I was still half tomboy and half all about the books and education.

I advise you if you are a parent of an Aries or any sign, have the talk. The knowledge I got about sex was from my friends and it was ridiculous. We had sex education at fifteen and I still had no idea what they were talking about.

Aries teenagers are curious about sex at an early age. If you don't tell them about it, they will find out misinformation. Even if you try to keep them from doing anything, chances are they will find a way to try it. I suggest being open with them about sex and the pitfalls of having sex early. The best information I received was from school, but I didn't understand a word of it. Sex education classes are useful, but a discussion should be had with one's parents. I never understood why my parents didn't talk about it but now I know it was because they were uncomfortable.

Even though I had a lot of things going on in my head, I was more interested in reading than ever. I was able to find a bit of peace and quiet at home once my mother got a job. I spent hours in my room reading books about religion and history. I still had band, track, softball, and yearbook to keep me busy, but I had other things I was interested in, like sex. I also got a job.

Aries teenagers need to be busy. The best thing that happened to me was getting a real job working at Hofstra University. From there, I worked at a clothing store. I morphed out of my tomboy phase because now, I could buy the fancy clothes I wanted. I still had male friends, but I wasn't hanging out as much. Most of my time was spent looking for "the one."

I thought I found it at fifteen with a Capricorn, but a Virgo and Scorpio broke that up before it got started. My next failed relationship at sixteen was with a Libra who didn't take anything seriously. Finally, my high school sweetheart was a Leo and we had a relationship for seven years. When I graduated from college, we had different ideas about how we wanted to live and broke up.

We will go through a lot of relationships trying to find someone who understands us. As a teenager, we don't really understand ourselves. I was not a yes person, but I would do anything for my friends. I learned to say "no" in high school when my Pisces friend would monopolize my time and I didn't have time to do the things I liked to do. I was independent at a young age and collected friends.

My anger and aggression were a product of not being able to voice my opinion at home. I wouldn't voice my opinion at school, but I was happy to answer questions in class. I used my aggression playing sports. I got into a lot of fights in elementary school. Plenty. I mellowed out when I dated the Leo and spent most of our time enjoying each other's company.

Aries Women

We have been through it, haven't we? The guys I have dated have shown me off, tried to rule me, and tried to belittle me. Uh, no. Why do they want a strong woman and then when they get one have no idea how to treat her? What they fail to realize is that if I am telling you something, it is to help you. I don't do a lot of unnecessary talking. I want things to be easy. I am not trying to have any drama, ever. If I see that your level of drama is too much to bear, I'm out. I have too many special gifts to waste on someone who does not appreciate me.

We are looking for someone who genuinely appreciates us. I mentioned this before but only someone who grew up with us can really know us. There is some man who knew you when you were a kid that had a secret (or not so secret) love for you. That is the man you need to find. All these new people are not going to get it. They have no idea who you were and how you shine like a diamond now. You were shiny back then, but you have been polished now and deserve special treatment.

Aries get along with Leos, Geminis, Sagittarius, and Aquarius as friends and in relationships. These signs will give you your freedom and not be intimidated by your strength. Find one who is well balanced and whose energy is positive. A bad one will lead to violence.

We are comfortable with Taurus, Capricorns, and Scorpios. If you are a young Aries, these signs might bore you. As we get older and more settled and more concerned with stability and comfort, these signs are more appealing. If you have these signs in your birth chart and if they have Aries or another fire sign in their rising or moon sign, things will work out better.

Another Aries and a Libra together is a toss up. There may be too much in common or nothing in common at all. I suggest friendships with these signs. The romantic relationship will seem off balance. Someone will be too masculine, and someone will be too feminine. For instance, the Libra may be too feminine for the Aries. Or the Aries is too masculine. When I was married to the Libra, he would often say I was too masculine. I had never been told that in my life. He seemed too feminine. I like a more masculine man and he likes a more feminine woman. In my defense, as an intuitive cardinal Aries, if my man is lacking in an area, I will naturally do what he can't do.

Our personalities bought out the opposite reaction and neither of us was happy about it. It was an epic fail. We spent hours talking to each other before we started a relationship. We should have stayed friends. Our friendship was so good that we mistakenly thought we had enough strength to get married. We were wrong because things you have in a friendship are not the same things you need in a marriage. You can share jokes and fun as friends. In a marriage, there are times when you have to put jokes aside and the Libra didn't know how to do that.

Aries tend to have a significant influence in our relationships. We dominate. We like to be in control. I don't think anything is wrong with it. Until, the relationship ends. We don't realize how dependent we are in the relationship. We depend on that person to need us. When it's over, it's like the other half of our body is missing. And yet, it is a relief because we were doing way too much. We snap back well but why can't we find someone who sticks around? In my own experience, until I meet someone that I don't have to control, it will never work. Who wouldn't need to be controlled? Someone who has their shit together. Someone who doesn't need me to fix them and who wants me because they see my worth.

Another reason relationships fall apart is because we are so influential. Our significant other may not like the things we like but because of our dominant personalities, they pretend to like what we like. We seem so enthusiastic and excited that it is easy for some simpleton to get caught up. That is why a Libra man is terrible for us. He will agree to anything in the beginning. He doesn't seem to know what he wants. He can pretend for a little while and maybe he isn't pretending. Maybe he doesn't really know what he likes. When he figures it out, he will move on to the next. We need a strong man with a strong but gentle personality. A man who can stand up for himself without getting rattled by our argumentative nature. I have only seen a Taurus, a Scorpio, and a Leo capable of dealing with my shenanigans without getting ruffled.

I do not suggest relationships with Pisces, Cancers or Virgos unless again, you have these signs in your birth chart. A Pisces will get on your last nerves with the negativity. A Cancer will annoy you by being overly sensitive. The Virgo will get on your nerves because of the need for perfection. All three are not strong enough for you. Their common moodiness and negativity will drive you nuts, unless you have those signs in your birth chart or vice versa.

Someone who admired you when you started from nothing and then grew to be a tiger lily, will appreciate you. This person was a kid when you were a kid. They remember you when you were a tomboy or a girly girl, when you first got boobs, and didn't know how to approach you. They might have been your friend or watched you from afar. Maybe you dated this person in high school. I hope you find this person because you deserve true love.

We meet people who think they know us. If you haven't known me for more than five years, you don't know anything. If you don't listen to what I am saying then you missed the answers to the questions you will have later on like, "why did she leave me?" Remember when I told you I won't do too much more of everything and you not help me with the kid, the housework or the bills? Remember when I said, "You take me for a joke" or "when I'm gone, I'm never coming back?" I always have to show these ignorant dudes. Then, here they come, I won't even open the door.

Aries Men

Aries men are very masculine. They like to be in charge and that includes their relationships. I never really thought an Aries and Aries relationship would work but I guess it can if there is trust and someone is submissive. There must be balance in the relationship.

I have known Aries who have had long term relationships with Cancer, Virgo, Libra, and Pisces. Why did these relationships work? I found that the Cancer, Virgo, Libra, and Pisces in these relationships allowed the Aries to be in charge. The Aries was the head of the household. The Cancer, Virgo, Libra, and Pisces in these relationships were happy being subservient to the Aries. If the Aries wanted the Cancer, Virgo, Libra, or Pisces to work, they did. If the Aries wanted the Cancer, Virgo, Libra, or Pisces to stay home, they stayed home. The masculine Aries did what he wanted when he wanted. Sure, the Cancer, Virgo, Libra, or Pisces cries or nags, but that's what the Aries expects from them. Their ultra-feminine behaviors work for the Aries because the Aries is the prime masculine.

An Aries who wants more of a challenge is compatible with Aries, Gemini, Leo, Sagittarius, and Aquarius. If he is looking for his equal, these signs are it. They will challenge you and correct you. They are independent and will expect you to respect them. The Aries men I know are very accommodating to their strong willed significant other. If you are not this type of Aries, you shouldn't even bother. The ones I know, respect their relationship and they seem a bit henpecked. They even become similar to their spouse. One man I know in particular, never used to talk about hunting and shooting. He got married to a Leo who seems to run the house and next thing I know, he is talking about hunting and shooting. He is in his fifties. Never believe an old dog can't learn new tricks. He can. Aries tend to become like their partners.

Taurus, Scorpio, and Capricorn are toss ups. They may work, they may not. An Aries man may find these signs to be deceitful. They are not as outspoken when it comes to what they want. They are reserved in relationships and this may put the Aries man's fire out. He doesn't understand someone who is patient. He doesn't understand the inability to say what is wrong. Unless, he has these signs in his birth chart, this will be a very frustrating relationship.

Aries Parents

Aries love their children. We take pride in our children. We tend to be over protective. We watch everything our kids do. We are their biggest cheerleader. We look at them as little pieces of ourselves. It takes some time for the Aries parent to realize that our children have their own minds and are their own people. I didn't know what I was doing as a parent. I remember having to revise my parenting behaviors as I saw what type of child I had. All children are not the same and can't be treated the same.

Aries are very similar to children and children are drawn to us. Strange children want me to hold them wherever I go. Their parents look at me oddly because I don't have a friendly face. It doesn't make a difference to children, they want me. I am the piped piper of children, the elderly, and animals. I talk to them all the same. I speak to children, the elderly, and animals. I don't baby talk babies. The angriest and fussiest children will come to me and no one else. I have been in stores and if I don't acknowledge the child, it will cry and scream. It's probably why my son and I got along so well when he was a baby.

Aries are attentive and observe everything. I knew when my son was getting sick and if he was in pain. I knew something was wrong when he started snoring at nine months. Babies shouldn't snore. We found out he needed his adenoids removed.

Aries want to do things our parents didn't do. I told my son I loved him every day. I spent a lot of time with him. I wanted him to be able to tell me anything. As an Aries, I'm a bit of a penny pincher so I didn't buy him everything he wanted. I spoiled him with love and attention but not material things. I like to travel so I took him places. Wherever I went, we would visit the zoo, the museum, the conservatory, and the abortorium.

Aries can be good disciplinarians and can go overboard. We don't want our kids to get into trouble. We want to protect them and keep them safe and the way we understand this is for them to behave in public. We forget what it's like to be a kid who wants to explore and test everything in our surroundings.

My instinct was to treat him the way my parents did. I grew up in the seventies, but my son was growing up in the late nineties. I tried to spank him for whatever the teachers said was going on in school. They called me just about every day. It was getting to the point where I thought I would have to quit my job. Finally, I gave up. There had to be a better way to handle this.

I told him if he told me what he did and what the teacher did, he wouldn't get in trouble. The thing is I had no idea who was lying. Eventually, I would wind up going to the school to see what was going on. I am an active parent. I am involved in my son's life. I want to know what is going on. In an ideal world, I wouldn't have worked when he was growing up.

My son had a lot of energy growing up. When he was four, I signed him up for sports. He played a sport or two until he graduated from high school. I went to every practice and every game. I am proud of my son. I was smart enough to know that I wasn't going to be able to give more than one kid my full attention, so I was responsible and only had one. I wish I had been smarter about my choice of father for him, but you live and learn.

I made mistakes but I know my son knows I love him. Aries parents are good providers and they will do what they believe is best for their kids. My father, who was an Aries, was the same way. We got spanked if we were out of line, but he was fair, everyone got an ass whipping.

Aries in Relationships

Why do Aries get so angry? It is because we are extremely nice. Yes, that ball of fire learned from an early age that people will use us. People will take the Aries kindness for granted. You know that person who buys you lunch, or gives you a Christmas present, or babysits your kids without getting paid? Probably an Aries. We don't mind loaning people money or treating them to lunch. We remember your birthday and will take you out. We are the friend who picks you up when your car breaks down, who picks your kids up from school because you can't, or who will go visit your sick mother.

In the beginning, we bring gifts everywhere we go. We don't mind paying the tab. Unfortunately, that same kindness is not returned. People begin to expect us to pay for things and to bring gifts. We are cheerful about it for longer than we should be. Sometimes, we don't stop because we accept the role when it comes to our relatives.

When it comes to loaning money, that is a practice I urge you to stop if it keeps you from paying your own bills. I know Aries who have paid for their siblings to go to college and put off having a family. We will sacrifice ourselves and our wellbeing for others in a heartbeat. If this is you and you are able to have a life and help others, by all means continue. There is nothing better than giving charity and it will make you feel better if you do it in the spirit of knowing you will never get it back in return.

Aries are givers. One of our gifts is the ability to sow seeds. We are the astrology sign that brings great ideas and creativity to others. We start as children and even if we are not nurtured to do this, we will naturally do it. An Aries that feels good about himself or herself always feels better giving.

Aries are natural givers. We don't need anyone to tell us to share. Our spirit of giving gets entangled when we start getting in relationships. We overdo it when we are teenagers until we get burned. We give in every relationship. If we have nothing to give materially, we give sex and emotional support. We allow ourselves to be drained. It took me a long time to stop giving myself completely. I'm still not sure if I've mastered that.

If we think someone is worthy, whether he is or not, we will support that person financially. We want to see the good in people because we know we are good (but we learn later that does not mean that other people are good like us). It will take some of us years, to stop funding people who are not worthy. Who's not worthy? Someone who lives with you but doesn't work, who eats the food from your table and the table of your children, who spends her money on clothes and hair when bills need to be paid. Inconsiderate people, able bodied people who can work but don't, and people who aren't contributing.

Aries give too much in relationships. It's like needy people can smell us. We take in the homeless, the needy, and the lost. We will raise a dead relationship from ashes. We put too much energy in it because we want love and we want someone to love us the same way. Turns out, no one loves us the way we love them. The best thing we can ever do is to start loving ourselves.

How should we manage all of this love energy? We turn that love on ourselves. Massage your own feet, tell yourself how wonderful you are, and pamper yourself. Everything you do for that other person, do for you. The more you love yourself the more the right person will be attracted to you. Forget about pleasing someone else for a minute. Concentrate on yourself.

I was married twice to two people who needed me. I thought I loved them. I thought that by taking care of them, they would love me. They did not. Someone has to love you for who you are and not what you can do for them. How can you tell if you have someone who loves you for you? Don't do anything except spend time with them. Don't buy them anything, don't move them into your house. Someone should be able to love you and you should be able to love them and spend time together doing nothing.

Find someone who wants you but doesn't need you. Shit is different now. Everyone should be taking care of themselves. If you have to step in to "help" someone, think twice. If you haven't established a connection with the person before you start taking financial responsibility, chances are, you will not be appreciated. You are better off helping people you are NOT in a relationship with, believe me. The minute an Aries gets their heart involved, we are doomed.

Think about when you were in high school. You had nothing. Most of us had relationships and we didn't have to give them anything. Now that we are adults, use that same thought process when you pick your next relationship. We have to stop trying to win people over with stuff. Who is this person and are we compatible? That is what matters in the end.

You shouldn't have to move anyone into your house or apartment. This person should be able to date you and live in their own place. You shouldn't have to help this person with rent, and you should be able to pay your own rent. After some time, if a person likes you, they will want to do things for you because they value you as a person.

You hear a lot about Aries chasing. Let me explain that. We initiate. We will let you know we are interested but you will have to pursue us, or we will let someone else have a chance. If we are in love, we may go to the extreme. That's never a good look for us.

We fall in love fast, but we fall out just as fast. That's not love. We get infatuated with looks, money, talk game, and potential. When the potential is there, we hang on longer than we should because we have hope that eventually, the person will do the right thing. They never do. This is why loving yourself is so important.

We can seem nonchalant and unbothered. Most of us do not wear our hearts on our sleeves because we have been burned by love. Our pride is strong. We keep our emotions under wraps until you disrespect us, and we lose it. We like to feel like we are rescuing someone. We like to be in control. Aries are challenging and we will challenge every sign we date.

I had two Aries men approach me for a relationship. It did not go well. When I hear men say things like, "Don't you think you should be quiet?" "Why don't you do…?" "I think you should…," I lose my cool. I'm getting angry thinking about it. I am not one to be talked to like that by anyone. Who is he talking to? He doesn't even know me, we just met. I don't have time to even tell him how crazy he sounds to me. I'm out.

The other one lied about his whole life. I was like, "Wow." I give him credit for coming clean, but it was too late. I like the mild Aries more than the aggressive one. I guess because I am aggressive. Both of us can't be aggressive.

I can honestly say that the only time I have even considered being submissive is when someone I was interested in had three things: he was financially stable, he didn't need me to help him, and he listened to my advice. The three signs that came close were Taurus, Leo, and Scorpio.

People say Aries look sneaky. I'm always offended. I would defend myself to the core. I speak my mind so how am I sneaky? What they notice is that I think a lot. I like to have a plan but that doesn't mean I intend to cheat or steal your money or burn you in your sleep. I'm thinking of what to say, what to do, and how far to push the envelope. In that respect, my over thinking looks sneaky. I embrace it now. I do this in every aspect of life and that includes relationships. If I have a decent guy, I'm thinking about our next vacation. If you suck, I'm thinking about how to get you out of my life. I've had to move, change cars and change phone numbers to get away from exes. It's far better for me if the dude breaks up with me or I convince him that leaving is the best thing to do. I don't like drama.

When I was younger, I did not mind drama. If reacting to someone's bad behavior is drama then, I had drama. I always have a reason for my actions. I'm not flipping out because I am imagining something. I'm one of those people that if I work two jobs, you should work two jobs. My man should do what I am doing. As an older Aries, I've had enough of drama to last a life time. I can laugh about some of that stuff now.

Have I been hurt? Sure. Have I hurt people? Of course. It is far better that I break up than try to stick it out with someone I can't stand to look at anymore. I did you a favor. If you left me, you did me a favor. I believe that if something is supposed to work out, it will. If it isn't, it won't. I don't come to these decisions easily. I have run them over in my head a number of times. I've thought of every possible outcome.

The dream person for an Aries is someone who worships us and who we respect. Without the respect, it doesn't matter how much you love us. In the end, respect is a big deal breaker for us. I think that is why my last relationship ended in all honesty. The Libra didn't respect women and it took me a while to realize it. I would have stuck it out and gone to counselling with him, but he wanted to be with another woman and there was no point in trying to work on a relationship if someone else has caught his eye. I'm not going to say he cheated but he spent a night out at a cousin's house, and he had never done that before, so I think he did. Trust gone.

I didn't argue or ask him anything. I didn't care because I saw the writing on the wall when he stayed out. I am at the point now where if someone does something wrong that's on them. I respect my body and my health too much to try to get revenge. If you cheat, I am not cheating to pay you back. If you lie, I am not going to start lying. I don't imitate fools. I lead myself.

Aries go into relationships with lots of hope. We hope this person is the one who can hang in there. Our most valued asset is a good relationship. We can be both introverted and extroverted, so we need someone who can handle this. Aries needs someone who is not threatened or intimidated by us. We tend to jump in full force, but we should take our time (speaking from experience).

Aries wants to know they are important. I can't be second best. Aries put their significant others first and we expect the same respect. The minute I feel like I am not important in your life, I am backing away.

You get what you give with us. It is unconscious. We are a reflection of our closest relationships. We don't necessarily act like you, we return the energy people give us. If my husband is ignoring me and I ask him what is wrong but, he tells me to go away or that he doesn't want to talk about, I will leave him alone. If two days later, I am upset about something. I am not going to share it because I will feel that he doesn't care. Why? Because he couldn't open up to me, therefore, I will not open up to him. It's childish so why would I do this? If I notice that he can't be vulnerable, I won't be. Our survival instinct is strong. I will begin to think, why can't he share his feelings? Now, I have to hold my cards close to my chest because maybe he is not being honest with me. This is part of our over thinking, but it is our method of protection. Are we that sensitive? Yes, we are. You won't know but we notice everything.

Let's say the husband tells me what is bothering him after a few hours or a day later. He shares what made him upset. That would be a relief. All is forgotten. Let's say the husband never mentions what made him upset. Now, we are going to be suspicious. Don't believe me? Those are the things that we start filing away in our minds. If you are not an Aries, this may seem petty. It's not. It is the beginning of the end. We expect full disclosure. If I ask you what is bothering you, it's because I care so if I stop asking it's because I notice you are not receptive to being vulnerable. What else are you hiding?

Little things that you change in your behavior, we notice. I'm a tad bit different now, because I don't care as much. A person can shoot themselves in the foot a number of times, and I won't say a word. Eventually, the truth will come out and I won't have to say anything. I will ghost you, but you will know why. I don't like liars. I like to tell people up front what I am not dealing with and lying is one of those things. The only time I hold back is when I see that someone can't handle the truth. In my experience, Libras can't handle the truth and they start lying to protect themselves from it.

Aries Friends

We are good friends. The best. We lavish our friends with gifts, money, and time. We give the people we like the benefit of the doubt. We will trust you with our secrets and then, wham! We find out that our friends are not as loyal as we are. You have been talking about us behind our backs and telling our secrets. We are devastated. We didn't think you would do us that we because we are naïve. We make friends fast like we do everything else. A little bit of flattery and show us some interest and we like you.

I'm not like this. I am nice to everyone, but I am not everyone's friend. No one gets to know my secrets for a long time. I watch people before I let them into my life. When I was young, my teacher used to have me show the new kids around school. I was the person who made the new kids feel at home. I was nice. I hang out with a lot of people. But, I had only one best friend. Everyone else, in my head, no matter how many times we hung out, was an associate. I had a lot of associates until I find out they disrespected me in some way.

The reason I am slower to become fast friends is that my rising sign is Scorpio. I chose my friends and my mate with some hesitation. With that being said, my life is an open book but the only time my lips are sealed is when I am in a relationship. My relationships are private. I like to make sure the foundation of my relationship is solid before I let people know who I am seeing. I can change my mind about a person quickly and so, I don't have sex fast or make a commitment right away. I was slow before but after being betrayed by my ex, I'm even slower now.

Aries treasure their friends because we like to do things and we do these things with our buddies. We like to have someone to talk shit to and to joke with without being judged. It is good for our love interest to be our best friend. We like to have a love relationship with our best friend because it is more comfortable for us. Even if this isn't the case, friendships are important to us and it becomes harder for us to make solid friendships the older we get.

A lot of times, we are friends with people we grew up with or family members. We make new friends easily but most of them are only fair weather because we ask a lot of our friends. Our friends need to be available at a moment's notice. We like to talk about things we are going through, but we don't necessarily want you to give us a solution. We need someone to listen and have our back. Sometimes, that means, you can't ask any questions and just take a ride with us to spy on the ex-boyfriend. Or to drop us off on his block so we can sneak in the bushes and peek into his window to see who he's sleeping with. Or to have you call his phone or his job to see if he answers.

Aries friends will have you on an adventure, just don't let them get you killed. It's okay, we know you are scared. You're supposed to be. If you want to leave, speak up, otherwise you will catch it if we are in the middle of something and you chicken out. Aries get pissed with their friends when they try to stop us from doing something. Don't worry though, we won't be angry for long.

A friend has to be a positive influence because even when things are negative, we don't want to dwell on it. We know the bad side of any given situation. We don't need to be reminded of it. That is probably why Virgos and Cancers or anyone who can't see the bright side, can't be our friend for long (unless the sign is in our birth chart). Aries will not notice it at first or even overlook it. After a while, it will begin to irritate us. I don't care how mean we look or how bad life is, we don't want someone bringing us down all the time. The older we get, the more obvious it will become to you, Aries.

The thing about Aries is that we overdo it. We are too generous, too nice and too forgiving, until we are not. It takes a toll on us. We always remember birthdays and anniversaries. An Aries is lucky if they have friends and family who reciprocate. Usually, we don't. It's ok. Buy yourself gifts. Treat yourself to dinner or takeout. Donate to charities. Volunteer your time to a charity.

My friends become very protective of our friendship. They want to believe that I am their only friend. They become jealous of the other people I hang with. This happens when I am friends with men or women. As I have gotten older, I have distanced myself from having too many friends. When I am married, I don't have male friends. It becomes uncomfortable. Even my female friends are jealous of how much time I spend with my husband. I had one female friend who was jealous of the time I spent with my son. People want to own me. They want me all to themselves.

Aries Negative Energy

Aries doubt themselves a lot. The way we talk to ourselves in our head is murder. No one talks to an Aries worse than an Aries. We have to learn to repeat positive affirmations. I thought it was corny when I was in my thirties, but some of us will mature into it. I've always thought of myself as a positive person because I don't waste time on nonsense. I don't want to hear any nonsense and you won't catch me standing around talking negative about people. I am too busy talking myself out of or into something.

We tend to view ourselves harshly. People don't know this because we appear very confident. That's because no one will ever see us sweat. We have a reputation to maintain. In the public, we are reserved, or we are loud. Whichever Aries you are, people think you have self-confidence because we tend to be opinionated.

We take on a large workload, we help others, and we learn to say no when we are pushed to the limit. There are some Aries who have these qualities but don't display them. There is a meek Aries, the lamb. This Aries is not aggressive or loud. Mostly, introverted and has the same loner instinct. I don't know these people. I hear stories about them but in my reality, I don't know one. Even the quiet Aries, gets loud. Even the Aries who has a shy side, is not shy around their friends. The Aries who stays to themselves is displaying typical Aries loner behavior. People think we are meek because we let things slide off our backs. I have been accused of not caring. I care but I will never let you know unless, I think it would make a difference.

This loner behavior, anti-social and this meekness is not something you want to have consistently. We have to get around people and socialize so that we can formulate new ideas and bounce ideas off people. It's good to have some "me time" but don't let it get out of control.

We can be true to our nature but the best thing we can do for ourselves is to have self-control. We have to work on controlling our anger and our sex drive (when we are single and sometimes, even in our marriage). Too much of anything is bad for a person. We tend to overdo it. It took me having my son to control my temper. It took years for me to start meditating to stop the negative self-talk and the over thinking. I use exercise and meditation to slow the sexual appetite. Yet, when I get into my new relationship, I hope old dude can keep up!

Aries are always thinking. We spend a lot of time thinking. We need to learn to remove all thoughts from our heads and to relax. I meditate. It helps but you have to do it every day. It teaches you to clear your mind and to focus on breathing. Aries should do it in complete silence. I suggest silence because we are easily distracted by music and the full effect of the meditation is better in silence. Believe me, it will work wonders. Google it.

Aries have a lot of energy and we should exercise as much as possible, even if it is taking moments out your day to do deep breathing exercises. Walking is good to do. If you really want to destress, weight lifting is great. Yoga works well for people who don't want to go to a gym. You can find yoga instructions on television and on Instagram. People have mentioned to me that I should take up boxing, it is a good way for an Aries to release our aggression without beating people to a pulp.

Anything Aries can do to keep ourselves from over thinking is positive. Doing yoga at night is good for helping us to get sleep. I always exercise at night and my friends thought it was weird. I do it because it makes me exhausted and I pass out. I would ride the exercise bike at home or do a few yoga poses. I sleep well. We need our rest. I have gone a day without sleep but that is as far as I can go and still be able to function. If I only get a few hours during the week, I have to make up for the loss on the weekend.

Aries Gifts

Aries have great intuition. Some of us live by it. If my body says stay home, I'm staying home. If someone's vibe doesn't feel right, I am cutting them loose. If someone has a weird smell (and I am not talking about body odor), you got to go.

I met a guy once who smelled like death. I can't explain what that smells like, but it is pungent. It made me want to throw up. I took his phone number and had a couple of random conversations with him on the phone, but I never hung out with him. I hadn't heard from him in about a month or two and called his house. His father screamed at me in the phone, "He is dead!" And slammed the phone down.

I asked around to see if it was true or if maybe his dad was tired of girls calling the house. I have told my mother to tell guys I was married or dead if they called our house for me when I wasn't interested in talking or dating them. Anyway, I found out that he was dead, but no one told me how he died. It's still a mystery to me.

I've met wife beaters, killers, and other shady characters. I avoided them all because they did not sit well with my energy. How do I know? They have beaten, killed and done some really shady stuff to other people and I found out later.

Aries people need to listen to their inner voice except if it is telling you kill people or hurt yourself. You may be schizophrenic or have a mental illness, all jokes aside, get that checked out.

Aries are creative. We can solve most problems but use that for yourself as well as others. We are always helping other people to figure out how to better their lives and to fix their problems, we need to fix our own lives too.

Aries creativity stretches into our life on all levels. We are creative in relationships because we tend to get bored quickly. We motivate people and inspire. We don't even know we are doing it until someone tells us. People will tell you that something you did made them go after what they wanted. I like to hear things like that. All of the negative comments that I hear are nothing compared to the one time someone tells me something positive.

Every job I've worked, I have come up with some innovative idea. Some way to streamline the work load or to organize the office. I like doing that. It is fun to me. I have come up with ideas and people have stolen them. I am not upset. If it helped to make someone else's life better, good for them. I am never going to run out of ideas. I have been gifted with that. Find out what makes you happy that doesn't involve sex, drugs, or alcohol. You might like wood carving, playing piano, fishing, bowling, or whatever.

Aries are the initiators and we are supposed to start things and watch it grow. Our challenge is to complete what we start, one thing at a time. I know, we have so many things going on. As I am writing this, I have twenty other novels waiting for me to publish. At least, they are done. Some of them are from 2003 and others from 1994.

People like to copy us. Let them. They are not us. Copying is a form of admiration. But if it is your art or your writing or your project, get it copywritten and get it done. Get compensated for your work.

Things We Need To Work On

Yes, we are great. We are the first sign of the zodiac, but we need to work on some things. The most important things are our temper, our impatience, and our aggressiveness. Once we are in control of these three things, we cause less stress on ourselves. For an Aries, this would make us the best we can be and who doesn't want to be the best?

For the Aries who still has a bad temper, please understand, this is the worst quality to have as a person. It will get you in needless arguments. You will say the wrong thing to the wrong person. There are so many ways this can change your life for the worst. This may sound silly but counting to ten before popping off is helpful. Checking your surroundings is also a good thing to do. Make sure you have the right information before you lose your temper. I don't know how many times, I jumped to conclusions and went OFF. I learned early to get the facts and then determine whether it was worth getting upset. It wasn't until I had my son that I realized how important it was not to lose my temper. I didn't want him to see that side of me.

Being impatient will get you into trouble as well. Our impatience translates to speeding, running lights, and interrupting people. I haven't learned how to stop interrupting people. Slow talkers still drive me nuts. I'm better than I used to be. I like people who get to the point. I can listen to them all day without interrupting. Patience is hard to learn so I started meditating. It helps me to be silent. It helps me to think slower and move slower. I am forty-nine so it took me a long time to get to this point. I started in my forties. Don't wait to get to forty to start slowing down. I have had to pay for being in a rush with all the speeding tickets I've gotten over the years.

Being aggressive with people is not a good trait either. That too can get you into arguments and fights. Yelling your point or shoving people is not the answer in an argument. Sometimes, it's best to listen. Let the person be wrong. Let them say or think what they want to think.

Sometimes, people want you to be aggressive. Don't give them the satisfaction of saying, "See, look at her." They want you to make a fool of yourself. I'm no saint. I have grabbed things out of people's hands, snatched hats off heads, and kicked doors in. That may be fine as a younger person but as an adult that is immature and childish. At some point, Aries have to outgrow these behaviors.

Training yourself to remain calm, to become a listener, and observer rather than to react is the best thing to do. Practice yoga, meditation, or some form of exercise. We tend to let our energy rule us. We are supposed to rule over our energy.

Interactions with other signs

ARIES

It's easy to write about how signs interact but I would rather give you real examples of conversations I've had with other signs. I have friends, associates, and relatives of other signs and sometimes, I wonder if the way I interact with them is my individual behavior or is it how we, Aries, react to other people.

Aries are cardinal signs which means we don't hesitate to start something or to create change. We are rumored to not be able to finish things either but, we don't all fit in that category based on our birth charts and how we grew up. We are supposed to drop seeds, lead people to their destiny, and bring in karma. We are very creative, and we should tap into that aspect of ourselves, it keeps us out of trouble. We have cool and chill demeanors to maintain but having a little bit of nerd under our belt is good. Write your poems, create your music, write your books and draw those pictures. Go somewhere by yourself and leave the drama and the anger behind.

Our symbol is the ram. We are not goats, those are the Capricorn. We don't tend to follow anyone but our own instincts. Why is an Aries specifically identified with the ram? Rams are aggressive, they can climb mountains, and can jump twenty feet. This is important to understand because people don't seem to understand our determination. Aries take on tasks that seem impossible. Like the ram, this is part of our DNA. We don't have to think about climbing or jumping, we do it. It's in our actions that you will learn who we are as people. Aries don't brag. People call it bragging but if you listen, we are telling you how you can do it too. Our confidence is contagious.

Unfortunately, rams will bump heads but that is part of the relationship we have with each other. Every Aries, I have ever met, has challenged me in some way and after we learned more about each other, we became good friends or close associates. Some people can't handle our aggressiveness but most of the time, it comes out of frustration. If something is moving too slowly and we know we can get it done faster, we get aggressive. As we mature, we tend to manage our aggression.

Personally, I am bothered by slow talkers or people who can't get to the point. Spare me the details, please. I'm just going to interrupt you. I find a short cut for everything which includes my road trips, my work, and my chores. It's not because we like being rude, it's because we hate to waste time. A second wasted is a second we could be doing something else. When I realized how much time controlled my life, I had to learn how to meditate. I was always in a hurry and I seemed to always be out of breath. Even my anger was fast and furious, I was headed towards a heart attack.

Our keyword is I am. When I think of that phrase, it reminds me that sometimes, I forget who I am. As the first sign of the zodiac, we need to set an example for others, and we can't forget who we are, Aries.

People are watching us because we are always doing something. I try to make sure that what I am doing makes a difference. People are surprised by our sense of accomplishment. We tend to doubt ourselves and that is healthy in small doses, but we should never give up. You don't see rams giving up.

As a fire element, we represent heat. We heat things up. More importantly, fire spreads quickly. Fire, representing Aries, is not all bad or related to our temperament. We are warm hearted and loving. Like fire, we can warm a home with our love and devotion. Family is important to us and we will defend family with our last breath. Our warmth also spreads to strangers and people who need our help. We are very kind, too kind. Unfortunately, after we have been burned a number of times, we are less kind and helpful. We become more careful and aware of the wolf in sheep's clothing. We hide how much we care but the older we get the less we care. If we are not appreciated, we withdraw.

Aries are sensitive but we do not wear our sensitivity on our sleeves like Cancers do. You can't see our sensitivity on our face or hear it in our voice. As a masculine sign, we keep our emotions to ourselves. We let a few close friends know how we have been hurt but once it's over, it's over. We take it as a loss, and we move on. Aries will never forget when we have been hurt.

The thing about us is that we are leaders, so we are not going to do what the other person is doing in our friendships. If someone is being loud, we are going to be silent. If someone is acting like the bad guy, we are the good guy. We are individuals and natural competitors. We don't do it out of jealousy or envy. We do it because it is necessary. We can't have everyone doing the same thing. We don't like when things are the same. Someone has to be different. You will rarely find an Aries imitating anyone. If my best friend is drunk, I'm not getting drunk. If she is wearing red, I'm wearing black. I don't know about you, but I like to be different. If there's an all-black event, you can best believe my black outfit will be one of a kind and will fit me like it was made for me. We like to stand out.

In our relationships, it's a bit different. If you are an asshole; we are going to be a bigger asshole or ignore you altogether. You get loud, we will get louder or ignore you. You talk shit, we say shit that will hurt your tiny feelings. How do you beat a skilled warrior? You can't. Just when you think you know, we change up. We are going to figure out the thing that you aren't expecting us to do and we are going to do that. The thing that we know will take the wind out of your chest, we're doing that. The only time we won't is if we love you and we want to spare your feelings. If you never get it together and we have to let you go, whether we love you or not, we're going to tell you about yourself. This is why we are often known to represent karma. This behavior is natural to an Aries.

One of my friends growing up is an Aries. She was born two days after me, we were like sisters, but we were very competitive with each other. She always wanted to fight me because I was a bit taller, stronger, and smarter. We were walking down a busy street arguing about something. She said, "I wish you were my real sister so that we can get into a fight and still be friends after." I thought about it. "You know what, if you want to fight me, we can." I let her hit me first. I have brothers who punch like boys. Her punch did nothing, but my brothers have said that I am heavy handed. So, there we were fighting in the middle of the sidewalk. Some old dude saw us and told us we were too pretty to fight. After I released her from the headlock I had her in, we continued to walk to the park. She was mad and had a knot on her shoulder from that hit, but she got over it. Deep down though, I think she always resented me. I was taller and athletic. I was a tomboy and even though she was tough, she was more of a girly girl.

After we had our fight, and it was real, we continued to be friends. Aries are like that. We behave like boys in our relationships. We tend to fight or argue with each other to determine dominance and then, we can be friends. It never fails with the Aries women I have encountered. They test me.

I work with an Aries woman and when I first started the job, I believe she felt threatened by me and wanted me to know she was in charge. Truth is, she isn't in charge of me. She is knowledgeable at the job because she worked in the office for twenty-five years, but she definitely is not the boss of me nor is she my supervisor. I would have preferred if she would show me what I needed to know in a nice friendly manner, but that would have been too easy.

My Aries co-worker comes up to me holding an application with a coversheet I signed off on.
"Did you do this?"
I look at her, but I don't like her tone of voice. She is making it seem as if I had done something wrong. I looked at the document and saw that I had signed the coversheet, but I did not fill out the application, the vendor did. What I didn't like about her approach was that she was also talking loudly. I figured she was trying to intimidate me. She wanted me to know that she is smarter than me even though she hadn't been to college and I had. It was one of the reasons I was hired. She wanted me to know that she was not impressed with my college education.
"My signature is on it," I respond. She knows that, she can read. I continue working.
"Well, it's wrong," she says again loudly and officially. I am not sure what is wrong, but I scan the coversheet and see no errors. If she was referring to the application being wrong, then I was not responsible for that. Yet, I don't like how she is talking to me and I was not going to argue with her, and I didn't care what she was talking about. So, instead, I challenge her.
"Maybe, you did it," I say back to her loudly but without any emotion. I go back to

working on my project. She stood there with her mouth open in disbelief. She didn't know what to say and she walked off.

Sometimes, the best way to respond to aggressive people is to defer the argument back to them or to show disinterest. I still don't know what she thought was wrong with the application and I figured since she was more "knowledgeable" than I, she would make the correction. Needless to say, nine months later and we get along just fine. She approaches me with respect, and we carry on in a normal tone when speaking to each other. I'm not intimidated by anyone and if I am, you won't know. I am humble as well. I think she was expecting me to want her position and was feeling threatened by me. I am not in competition with anyone. I don't want her job and I am happy that she knows what she is doing. When I have questions, I ask her. Now that she knows me and I know her, we understand each other.

Before working with this woman, I had an Aries supervisor. The lady liked to argue, and she argued with everyone. The thing was, sometimes, she was wrong. I didn't mind telling her she was wrong, but I wouldn't argue with her. I remained professional. One day though, we had it out because she tried to say I did something that I didn't do, and I had enough of her trying to embarrass me. I didn't want to shout but she really was frustrating me. She shut the door AFTER the shouting match (and yes, we were shouting in the office for everyone to hear).

She said, "You are the only person who stands up to me and you don't take it personally." From my perspective, wrong is wrong. When I know a person's sign, I know exactly how to behave around them depending on our relationship. She is the supervisor, even though she could fire me or make my work day hell, her biggest concern is looking inept in front of the other employees. I know that. My aim was to show her that I had her best interest at heart. I am helping her to be the best supervisor she can be. If she is smart, she will understand that. Some things are worth arguing with her about and some things are not. I would only engage if the situation was detrimental to the work environment.

I honestly wasn't mad at her for being a hot head when I found out her sign because I knew she didn't know she was wrong. She was being a typical Aries manager and did everything herself. I knew, I was going to hurt her feelings by telling her she was wrong. If I didn't tell her, she would look like a fool when she found out the truth and then, things would be worse in the office. I had to put myself in her shoes. You know, Aries people don't like looking like a fool. I would have preferred to tell her in the privacy of her office, but she preferred to make a scene.

She started coming to me asking for my opinion before she did stuff. I heard her once say to someone, "If Melony did it, I know it's right." I got a good reference from Helene when I left that job. Even her boss, was like, "I like how you work with Helene." Helene was definitely intimidating, but once she trusts you, she trusts you. You have to prove yourself. And she likes to argue. I don't mind arguing. I don't start arguments, but I do participate. She learned to talk to me in the privacy of her office. She changed a lot while I was there. A Virgo staffer said to me, "She doesn't act as crazy as she did before. She was crazy." She wasn't crazy, she didn't trust anyone. Most of the mistakes that had been made, she made but she didn't trust anyone to do the work for her until I got there. She had too much work on her plate and I was happy to help her out. I was promoted after three months.

My conversation with a male Aries co-worker went differently because he is a more laid-back individual and he doesn't try to assert his power. He is not threatened by me or my position. He might even find me attractive as men usually do. He tells me one day that a hysterical vendor called him saying she needed her application approved. The vendor was late turning in her paperwork so he asked me if I could rush it, but, "I'm not going to turn it around in a day. That woman pissed me off. Can you believe she tried to report us because she didn't get a reminder notice?"

"What? The vendor is responsible for getting the application in regardless of the reminder. Hell, after a year, they should check on their own accord, especially if they are working on a project that is about to expire," I respond.

"I'm so pissed," he said but I couldn't tell from looking at him. I did overhear him talking on the phone before he asked me to rush the application. He did sound upset but he didn't blow up. I did the coversheet and filed the data. I gave him the coversheet and the application, but he didn't approve it until two weeks later. The Aries man is a hard worker and skilled but blaming him for something you did wrong is a bad move. He will lose his temper, but he will still get the work done but it won't be done when you want it, it will get done when he gets it done. Most of the Aries men I know can laugh things off. He can find the humor in regular nonsense.

When something gets under my Aries co-worker's skin, he doesn't have a problem saying it. He went into a rage when he saw the video of some girl licking ice cream in Walmart, that pissed him off! He had choice words for that idiot. You would have thought she killed someone. All Aries have a quick temper because some things really irritate us. Stupid stuff irritates us. As we get older, we need to choose our battles and not get so irritated with small stuff.

This reminds me of my father who was born March 25th. This man worked two jobs religiously, he never missed a day. He was a quiet Aries and I saw him get angry maybe twice. His anger wasn't loud anger like mine, he was a quiet attacker. I am a "scream at the top of my lungs" as a warning that you need to get away from me.

My father didn't give any warnings. My Aries male co-worker is also a March Aries and the biggest difference that I have noticed is that March Aries is the quiet warrior. My dad didn't do much talking. He talked about work, about the books he read, and history. He read a lot and had gone through a lot in life. The most notable thing about him is that he was a great provider. If you didn't start any trouble, there wouldn't be any trouble. He wasn't afraid of trouble.

We lived on Long Island and had a few relatives that lived in Harlem in the seventies. We went to visit them, and they lived in a crowded neighborhood. I won't say it was a bad neighborhood but there were dudes hanging around the street everywhere. The apartment was hot, so we went to sit on the apartment steps with my dad. When we got outside about five dudes were leaning on his station wagon. My brothers and I looked at each other because my dad was funny about people leaning on his car. We couldn't lean on his car and we were his kids. Our father finally made it down the steps because there was no elevator and our cousins lived eight flights up. He saw those guys leaning on his car and started smiling, not a good sign.

He was out of breath, but he walked over to the guys and said, "You see the car you're leaning on? It's mine. No one gets to lean on my car but me," and he leaned on the car.

"Sorry, man. We didn't know," said the guys and moved their conversation down the street. Let me mention, my dad was a big guy who grew up in Queens, New York and he wasn't afraid of much. I've seen this man confront groups of angry men with a bat and he didn't have to use it. He wanted to be a police officer, but he had a criminal record. I always wondered about that. The rumor was he killed a man. Back then, you couldn't search a person's criminal record online so I guess we will never know now that he has died. Watch out for those quiet people because you never know what kind of anger they may be holding inside.

As for my female Aries, I have April Aries females in my family and the thing that we all have in common is that we will speak the truth. People do not like it, but we will say what needs to be said. One of my aunts outed a pedophile in the family. Boy, did she rub some people wrong. I didn't see the problem. I was more bothered that no one did anything about him. Some relatives hated to see her coming, I loved her to death. At family reunions, she would call people out. I loved to sit right next to her. I could see myself in her role in a year or two, sitting at the family gathering, snitching on bad behaviors, and shameful misdeeds. Not really. I don't like the negativity so I will be at home minding my business.

Aries tend to be loners because we have been burned. It could be that we don't forget when our friends or family does something we don't like. We may have noticed that because we let things slide, people we are close to continue to repeat these behaviors. Once we get fed up, it's over. We like having someone to trust but if we don't, we don't.

We know that even when things are bad somehow, we survive. We are stubborn in that we will refuse to be around people after we have been betrayed too many times. Too many times to an Aries can vary from 1 time to 20 times. It doesn't take much for us to throw in the towel because our tolerance for bullshit is low. Some people can deal with the faults of others longer than us, good for them. They probably have a lot of fake friends. We would rather not hang around fake people who are talking about us and spreading lies. If we are business associates, we don't care because you need us as much as we need you to get the job done and we will allow you to know very little about us. We are masters at tolerating people we don't like if we need to get paid. We like money and money likes us. As for close friends, the circle is very small.

For the most part, Aries are bad at lying. We only do it to protect people. I will lie if I know the truth will hurt someone's feelings unnecessarily. For instance, if I know someone likes something and I don't, I will say I like it. I know if I say that I don't like it, they won't want it anymore. Everyone's tastes are not the same and I can respect people's horrible tastes. I know they don't really want my honest opinion. Some of my friends want my honest opinion and I know their feelings won't get hurt. My Taurus, Scorpio, Aries, and Gemini people want my honesty. I can tell them anything. Libra, Cancer, Virgo, and Pisces pretend they want it but can't handle it when they get it. It destroys them. Capricorn, Aquarius, Sagittarius, and Leo act like they don't want it because they know everything, but they are listening.

I never lie when it comes to life or death situations. If my friend tells me her man is abusive and she asks me if she should stay with him, I'm going to tell her no. I don't care if they have thirty kids, if she is an at home mom, or if he is a cop. I will help her get the hell out of there. I would rather help people than hurt people and sometimes, tough love is more helpful than trying to be nice. I would lie to her husband about where she is staying because that is a lie I can live with. If I think brutal honesty is helpful, I will give it to you. I want the same, but it doesn't mean I will agree. We can agree to disagree.

TAURUS

I have a lot of Taurus friends. I like them because they never judge me, and I have done some ratchet things in front of my Taurus friends that I would never do in front of anyone else. Even the ones I am no longer close with have never uttered a word about my bad behavior. They are valuable friends to have. I can tell them anything. My Taurus female friends don't fight but everyone one of them have defended me verbally, to the death.

Tauruses are bulls. What kind of animal is a bull and how does this relate to the Taurus? Tauruses, like the bull, move slow and think slow. They take time to formulate their thoughts. It isn't until they are angry that things happen quickly for them. Fortunately, you would have to push and prod a bull, I mean, the Taurus to make him or her angry. They really want nothing more than to be left alone to brood. Tauruses brood. They want to know why other people have stuff. Tauruses like stuff. Their keyword is I have. They want stuff. They value people based on what they have, and they judge themselves this way as well. When you have a conversation with a Taurus, they spend a lot of time talking about what they have.

A Taurus may hate her job but will stay there for twenty years. A Taurus may be cheated on by her husband, but she won't leave him for a number of years. A Taurus can live through some terrible times. They are not quick to make any false moves. They are a fixed sign which means they don't make changes unless they have to. A Taurus can live with not being satisfied. They carry on. As long as a Taurus has all of their comforts like food, a nice home, a nice car, and luxuries, they will find a way to be happy. Security is important to a Taurus from an early age.

My Taurus ex-husband was a fighter under pressure. He doesn't like getting backed into a corner. The Taurus man is a true specimen of a man. He would defend and care for his wife. Tauruses are fixed signs which means they don't like change. They are stubborn and it takes a lot to change their minds about something. They don't judge you for your past mistakes and that is a thing of beauty for an Aries woman. We have made many mistakes, but we own them. A Taurus man is very manly but gentle. He can be rough as a brute, but it is only when he is pushed. He likes to take care of his partner and he likes to be comforted. He is passionate under the quiet reserve and watchful eye. He wants you to be happy and will work hard to make you happy.

The Taurus man is stable, loyal, but stubborn. When he decides he is going to do something, he does it. I have never met a Taurus man who hangs out with women unless he plans on being with that woman. They take relationships seriously.

I was married to a Taurus and it was a very comfortable relationship. He didn't argue, he was romantic, and he liked to play. It was one of the best relationships I've had but like anything, if it's not for you, it's not for you. I don't have anything bad to say about him. He paid the bills and he worked two jobs. He was a great role model for my son. Unfortunately, he got restless living in our small town. He wanted to move but that was not an option for me at the time.

A few months after saying he wanted to move, the Taurus lost his main job and that to him, was a sign for him to move. He wanted to move to Seattle. I was not going to move to Seattle. For me to move, he would have to have a job first. There should be a plan in place. The Taurus did not see it this way. He wanted to stay with friends until he got a job. I am not the type to sleep on anyone's couch. A Taurus is stubborn, once the mind is made up, that's it. I am not one to stop people from doing what they want to do. I know that if someone is dedicated to the relationship, they will do what's best for the relationship. He was not seeing it that way. Most people do what's best for them. Once I see that, I realize that I don't have the right to ask them to do otherwise. I had made enough sacrifices for the relationship so, if he couldn't wait a few years for us to travel together, then, he couldn't.

What I liked about the Taurus, his friends were his friends and they did not come to the house often. They would hold their conversations outside or elsewhere. I met his friends and they were respectful of our marriage. We went to gatherings and to visit friends and family. It didn't take up our whole life. We would get around them maybe once a month. The Taurus made our relationship the focus. He would invite me out on a date once a week. He was thoughtful and considerate.

The Taurus was a funny person. He would tell me about his day. His part time job was as a taxi driver which is funny because I had a Taurus aunt whose side hustle was as a taxi driver. Taurus people find other people interesting. They like to hear the gossip. You don't see them gossiping but they know stuff. Taurus are similar to us because they know a lot of people. They can easily make friends. They keep their friends for years even when they outgrow each other.

Most of the time, they ask me for advice. It seems that my Taurus brothers and sisters always find themselves in sticky situations. The thing about them, that is so different from Aries, is that their reaction to most things is calm. You have to work hard to make a Taurus explode. They have explosions but for the most part, they are cool and calm. I like this about them because many times when I was about to hype up a situation, I would look over at my Taurus friend and she would be unmoved. It calms me down.

Once when I was working as a teacher, we had a teacher's appreciation day and they provided us with food. We went into the lounge after the ceremony and there was fruit on the table. Three of us, started eating the fruit because we thought they had put the leftovers in the teacher's lounge. Another teacher came in and was so upset.
"You are eating my food," she said.
I was apologetic. I was telling this woman how sorry we were. I felt horrible.
My Taurus friend says, "how were we supposed to know all of that fruit belonged to one person. Who eats that much fruit?"
The Taurus got some more grapes and sat at the table.
Let me say, I was amused at her response and I didn't feel as guilty. If the Taurus wasn't there, I probably would have given the woman money to compensate her for the loss of her fruit.
The woman who put the fruit on the table said, "Why didn't you ask before you started

eating? The ceremony was in the auditorium. Why would food be in the teachers' lounge?"

The Taurus was so calm that I stopped stressing because situations like this normally stress me out. The Taurus said, "it was a mistake." And it was. Now, my view began to shift. I was blaming myself for not being more careful but now, I was wondering why the woman was so upset. It was an accident. No one was trying to eat her food on purpose, and we had no idea it belonged to anyone. The other woman who had eaten the fruit with us went to the auditorium and got the lady some more fruit but let me tell you, we all were wondering why she was so upset. She must have been famished. I am going to guess she was a Cancer.

I mentioned that Taurus people will ask me for advice, but they won't necessarily take the advice. My friend likes to ask me, "what would you do?" But she never does what I do. I like that about her because she is her own person and is not trying to be like me. I know a lot of people that I have been friends with, that wanted to be like me. Eventually, they irritate me, and I stop hanging out with them. I like people who are themselves.

My Taurus friend has been unlucky in love but in a different way from myself. I would say she has been lucky because she has never been married when I have been married twice, unluckily. I like being married and she says she wants to be, but I am starting to believe that she doesn't. My friend is independent and when she dates, she wants a man who will help her pay bills and do stuff around the house. My priority is to find someone who appreciates me, and the other stuff is secondary.

She dated a guy for over five years, and he was seeing another woman in another state when she met him. He proceeded to date both of them. I told her that I didn't think he was the right guy for her, but she said they were friends more than in a romantic relationship.

Soon they decided to see each other exclusively and he told her he had stopped seeing the other woman. The truth was that he hadn't. She asked me what I would do and I, of course, told her to leave him. If you can't cut him off, be friends but don't have sex with him. He was still having sex with the other woman, she saw texts messages to prove it.

My Taurus friend calls me crying after a few months of being "exclusive" with the guy who happens to be a Leo, "Mel, what am I going to do?"

"What happened?"

"The Leo is cheating again. This time it's with a woman who has a kid."

"How did you find that out," I asked? I wasn't surprised.

"I went through his phone when he was sleeping. I figured out his passcode. The woman was asking him when he was coming over and if he was going to give her money for her son's school clothes. He doesn't even give me money for the bills, and he stays here all the time," she cried.

In my own defense, I hear about this man's shenanigans often and I don't know why anyone would put up with his behavior unless you are cheating too. Or you don't care, or your self-esteem is low.

As an Aries, the only time I put up with this type of relationship was when a Gemini guy told me he wasn't ready to settle down. I wasn't seeing anyone, but I was looking. If the Gemini wanted to hang out with me and I wasn't seeing anyone, I would. We were not exclusive, and he was honest about what he wanted. So, I didn't understand how my

Taurus friend was staying with this Leo when they were supposed to be in a relationship. I don't like dealing with liars. I value honesty.

"Listen, I don't know why you are still with him. I guess when you get tired, you will leave," I said.
"Why is he like this?" She asked. This went on for more than five years, maybe seven.

Eventually, she broke up with him, but she hung in there through a lot. Taurus are loyal and they are good friends. The only thing I notice is that they doubt themselves and tend to have a low opinion of themselves. Their depressions can last for years. Once they regain their self-worth, they are able to achieve a lot of positive accomplishments.

My friend is a great artist and does a lot of art work for local businesses. My other Taurus friend kept her job for a number of years and became part of the management team. I wouldn't be surprised if she becomes the CEO in the near future. My ex-husband moved to Seattle and got a really good job with a fortune five hundred company. He was able to purchase a home. As a legal immigrant from Egypt, this is a big deal.

GEMINI

Geminis are my favorite people. You can't hold them down and they are always down to party and have fun. They like to travel and go out but like us, they need to recharge. What is different about them is that even though they like to be in a relationship, they don't make it the end all or be all like we do. When they are not in a relationship, they don't get depressed about it. They are surrounded by enough friends that they only feel the loneliness when they are home recharging. Soon, they are back partying, and all is forgotten. A lot of my Gemini friends are bachelors or bachelorettes.

If anyone can keep up with an Aries, it's a Gemini but can we keep up with them? Geminis are the Twins because they are always of two mind sets. For the ones I know, it's either work or party. The work hard and play harder was either describing a Gemini or was a phrase a Gemini created to describe his life. They always seem to have a lot going on. They spend a lot of time thinking but mostly about what to wear to the party. What to drink? Who to invite? Or they are thinking about how many additional hours to stay at work. How much money will I make if I pick up another job? How can I make extra income? I am sure they think about other things but those are probably typical thoughts.

Not only do they have a dual mind set, they also have dual behaviors. One minute, they are joking and the next, dead serious. They can be the boss, one minute and your buddy, the next. It happens fast.

Geminis are mutable which means they are flexible. They have all kinds of friends. They like different races and nationalities. They see all people as a potential friend. The Gemini I've known for over twenty years is Jordanian. He knows people from everywhere and I like having him as a friend. The same goes for my uncle who has friends of many races. He would introduce my family to his new friends from college. You never knew who he would bring to the house. Geminis are air signs who value their freedom. Geminis move freely among people, from job to job, and from place to place. Like air, Geminis are everywhere. The Geminis I know travel and experience other cultures.

Geminis are smart even if they don't get a lot of education because they like learning new things. They do research and listen to what other people tell them. If a friend is into art, they will learn about art. If a friend is an excellent cook, they will spend time learning and observing what the friend is cooking. They are not imitators and so, they will create their own recipes.

Geminis like Aries because they know we are smart. I have a relative who is a Gemini and his thing is to correct you even when you are right by saying the same thing in another way. He must be the authority on all things. Some Geminis are threatened by our intelligence. People are afraid to admit our intelligence. I'm not sure if it's because we don't seem to care or because we are very confident.

Sometimes, though, we can say something dumb and right behind it, say something profound. They don't like that. This gives Geminis a bit of trepidation about us. For instance, they like to talk to us in private rather than in public. Our one-on-one conversations with Geminis can go from a wide range of things. They like gossip and we like to listen. Also, we can be silly around them and that is where they get a little nervous. Aries can take silly or crazy to another level and it worries Geminis because although, they can lose it, they don't know

how to handle us when we lose it. They
don't know if we are playing or for real.
Even though Geminis like to have fun, they
are serious people. They always have one
foot in reality because of their dual spirit.

My supervisor is a Gemini. He doesn't know
if I will say something smart or if I will say
something off the wall. There are days
where I am tired, and I am only paying half
attention rather than the full attention I need
to pay. When I say something great, he is
pleased. A lot of times, he will consider
what I said and have a private conversation
with me to see if my idea has any value. If
we are in a meeting, he will cut me off
because I am a bit long winded and he is
afraid of where I am going with the topic.
He will even try to rush me. Usually, other
people want to know what I am going to say,
so I get to finish. I'm going to finish
regardless, even if I have to bring it up later.
I like things short and sweet, he wants them
even shorter and sweeter. If anyone is going
to be long winded, it's him. What's funny is
that there are two other Aries in the office
besides me, and we all have out talked him
on occasion. Our meetings can last longer
than expected.

Like us, Geminis make things happen. They will make things work better and faster. Whenever I work with a Gemini, we get things done. Processes will be faster, things will be organized, and things will work better. We don't have time for cumbersome and burdensome deeds. I have better things to do. Every job I have ever had, I tailored the work to get done as fast and efficient as possible. I don't like slow things and neither do Geminis.

Some Geminis become bitter when they get older because they realize they have trifled away relationships and money for the sake of fun and freedom. This type of Gemini never became grounded. It is never too late for a Gemini to gain his or her footing. It will take dedication and patience which are skills Geminis must develop. It occurs mainly when they fall in love and want to have a family. They may never get to this point. A Gemini must find something more important than themselves. If he or she does not, they will always be a slave to their own whims and desires.

Geminis are mutable which means they are always moving around. You can't pin them down once they get started. They don't stay in one place for too long or in one relationship. Geminis are usually good cooks, they know good jokes, and they like music. Their interests are varied and uncommon. They fall prey to their own desires and will put their needs before the needs of others. The worst Gemini to be around is a low vibrating Gemini. Even though he will appear happy go lucky, his vibe will take you down. He will be overly enthusiastic to party, drink, smoke and have sex. He may force these things on you. A low vibrating Gemini can be cruel and divisive.

I had an off and on relationship with a Gemini for about twenty-years. He never wanted to settle down and is still a bachelor. When he did settle down the few times he got married, it was because he felt pressured to do so. As soon as he did it, he regretted it. He felt trapped. He says he will not to marry again. He tried twice like I did but unlike me, his urge to party is strong. He is a social butterfly which I am not. His bad boy behavior ruined a lot of his relationships. My personality is such that he wouldn't be able to live with me. I am too routine, and partying is not my life, it is more of something to do when on vacation. There is no way I can party every weekend with him. He is best suited for another Gemini who values freedom like he does. I imagine they would have a swinger type of open relationship and she would have to be wealthy to afford the way he spends money.

This Gemini would call me on Sunday after the clubbing was over and I got to see the aftermath of his weekends. He would have cracked teeth, swollen face, and scratched knuckles. Either he got into a fight with a person or he got into a fight with the ground. Either way, he was blacking out from drinking. He didn't do anything half way, it was all or nothing.

When sober, this man would cook dinner for me, and we would sit around watching movies. He never stopped talking. He talked about everything. Even then, I always felt that he was getting bored like he had other things on his mind. He would move around the room, he was in the kitchen, and in the bathroom. He wasn't still for long. As an observer, I knew he would irritate me more than I could stand if we were in relationship. We were better as friends without benefits. I had to remind him of that and eventually, he agreed.

I know a lot of single Geminis, male and female, and I am exhausted watching them.

They are always going out to eat, going to concerts, traveling, hanging out all night and dancing. Thinking about them makes me tired! But if I want to have fun, I'm looking for a Gemini.

When my Libra husband and I divorced, I went to hang out with a Gemini. A Gemini I grew up with asked me to come visit. I flew out and we partied all day and into the night. I haven't seen this woman in a number of years but when we got together, it was like we never separated.

I spent the evening and the early morning hanging out with her and some other friends I hadn't seen in years. Geminis know a lot of people and are the ones getting friends together. No one turns down a Gemini event. There will be fun, food, and drinks. Geminis have plenty of friends because they collect people. If a Gemini doesn't have a lot of friends, the rising sign or moon sign may be in a less gregarious sign.

Geminis will want you to spend all of your free time with them and will get upset if you do not. They will stop hanging with you if they believe you are a party pooper. The appeal of a Gemini for an Aries is their childlike behavior which we share. They are in touch with the fun side of life. Even though I like them a lot, I can only hang with them for a little while. I may be childlike, but I am not a child. I am a fully functioning grown up with responsibilities. Geminis behave like they have no responsibilities and some of them don't. They will do what they want regardless of spouse or children. This is the quality that gets them in hot water at work, at home, and in the street. A matured Gemini is one who has experienced a lot of hardships in life but has learned to balance his or her responsibilities with their self-interests.

When I divorced the Libra, the Gemini male friend called me up to ask me if I wanted to hang out. For him, the best way to get over something is to drink, do drugs, and have sex.

"I'm not ready to hang out and party," I said.
"You'll have fun. We used to hang out all the time remember?"
"That was twenty years ago. I'm not into going to clubs anymore. It's boring to me."
The Gemini was quiet for a minute, "Come to my apartment. I live in a new place. We can watch television. You'll like Kevin Hart's standup routine on Netflix." I hadn't

seen him in about nine years, so I was okay with hanging out at his place. Besides, I didn't think he would still be attracted to me. I wasn't the same young girl he remembered.

I get over there and the Gemini is in a robe. I laugh. "Were you planning on going out?"

"Sure, a little later," he says. He lights a joint. I feel like I am living in 1998. We talked about my marriage, his kids, his last relationship, and his rehab which clearly isn't working. I sat there for an hour as he paced around the room. He showed me around his apartment, and we ended up sitting on the balcony. I told him I needed to go because I don't like driving at night.

"Are you sure you don't want to have sex first?"
"No, I don't plan on having casual sex," I answered.
"But we are old friends. We know each other," says the Gemini.

"Thanks, but no." We knew each other. I don't know anyone anymore. People have disappointed me enough to know that I don't know anyone. I also know his lifestyle and it wasn't anything I was interested in. I wasn't interested in the past, I wasn't interested now, and will not be in the future.

"Maybe we can go to the movies or out to eat," says the Gemini.
"Sure." I wasn't going to hold my breath.

No hard feelings but I don't think the Gemini will ever outgrow his childish behavior and I am not going backwards. If I was some kind of good time girl who wasn't trying to get married to a quiet stable genius, I would hang out with him. I know that my rejecting him landed me on his party poopers list. It's ok, I'm an adult.

Geminis are good with children but may let them get away with doing things kids shouldn't do like drinking, smoking, and swearing. The Gemini is the fun aunt or uncle who won't tell your mother or father what you are doing. You can count on your Gemini aunt or uncle to supply the liquor or smokes and keep your secrets. Even so, Gemini's are hard on their own children. They want perfection.

CANCER

Cancer women seem to have a lot of problems. When I talk to them, they are always going through something terrible. One of my co-workers is a Cancer and just about everything that can happen to a person has happened to her.

One of my brothers is a Cancer and he is very supportive. I know a few other Cancer men and I don't have anything bad to say about them. I find them to be more interesting than the women and less whiny. The men tend to think before they speak and therefore, answering a question doesn't occur as fast as an Aries would like. Not everyone can be fast but for an Aries, this can be irritating.

Cancer's keywords are I feel. Let's explore this. The thing about Cancers is that they are always feeling. I don't think they are always crying but they are always upset because someone did not acknowledge their feelings. Everything bothers them because of this sensitivity. Yes, Cancers are sensitive. Nothing is wrong with being sensitive, but no one wants to hear about it every minute of the day. Not all Cancers talk about how they feel and those are the ones I like. The ones who are always mentioning how upset they are, upset me. I don't like being depressed. I don't like to be reminded about the ills of living. I like to move in positivity and so, I tend to avoid sad Cancers.

The symbol of Cancer is the crab. How do crabs represent Cancers? Crabs can be aggressive towards each other, they are active, they don't have a backbone, they burrow in sand or mud, and they walk sideways. Cancers tend to be shy but aggressive when they feel betrayed. I won't say they hid in the mud, but they don't bring unnecessary attention upon themselves. They aren't loud and obnoxious. They seem shy but they are comfortable with the people they know.

Cancers are not party people like Geminis, but they find enjoyment in things that they find interesting. This can be fishing, working out, or cycling. Their activities are usually things a person can do on their own. They don't build their lives around entertainment. They are comfortable at home like Tauruses, but they don't require all the luxury. The walking sideways represents how Cancers tend to sabotage themselves. They can withdraw from people and things because they got their feelings hurt. This is like taking one step forward and two steps back. Progress is slow for them. All Cancers are not like this which is why finding out what planets are in their birth chart is important.

I enjoy talking to Cancers because they have interesting problems. It is interesting to me because I don't suffer from those problems and I wonder how they are able to move around or work or do anything with so many ailments. Cancers like attention but Aries are stretched thin. We can't give them the time-consuming attention they need and that's when the worst comes out in a Cancer/Aries relationship. They start gossiping, everything is wrong, and they begin to imagine things that are not true. They begin to believe that people are talking about them and that no one likes them.

The truth is that once Aries gets tired of the attention seeking dependent Cancer, they bail. Typical Aries style is to tell you why things are not working. If you chose to ignore what we are saying, how is this our fault? Therefore, the Cancer thinks we don't care but in truth, Aries will avoid people who suck the life out of us and who don't listen to our warnings. Aries bad reputation comes from a Cancer, a Virgo, a Libra, a Capricorn, and a Scorpio (I'm sure a Scorpio doesn't care but they want revenge). They are the signs that spread rumors when they don't get what they want, or they don't know why someone doesn't feel the same way they feel. Instead of changing or letting it go, they make it about us. It's fine. We don't care. We gave you fair warning.

My moon sign is Gemini which means I am a talkative type and I can chat with anyone. I want to know everything if it's original. I give Cancers a platform because they want to be heard. The problem is that they never stop. Once they have your ear, you are their captive. You will be the person they come to tell their problems to, and they will always have a problem. My issue is when things get repetitive, I am no longer interested. Another problem is that when at work, I am not interested in personal problems. I like talking about work but not much else. When someone's personal problems become more important than work, I am no longer interested. I get annoyed. Everyone has problems but everyone is not at work complaining. I am not a fan of habitual complainers and whiners.

This Cancer co-worker is unusual because most of the Cancers I worked with were quiet and brood-ish. She broods but she likes to do it in front of an audience. I suspect she has a lot of Leo in her birth chart. Our daily conversations are unsettling for me because they require me to be extra sympathetic, which I am not. After two dead pets, I begin to wonder if a person is killing their pets. After two serious illnesses, I start to wonder if you are exaggerating or harming yourself. I understand that some people tend to get more unfortunate things happening to them in life, but it makes me wonder if maybe you are causing them. I have plenty of traumatic experiences, but I don't dwell on them. Some people like to dwell on their unfortunate circumstances.

Every time she goes to an appointment, I hear about it. If she scrapes her legs because she was climbing a ladder and cleaning her gutters over the weekend, I will hear about it. Anything that happens to her is a conversation. If no one listens to her describe her ailments, she is upset because no one notices her. We notice. If someone offends her sensibilities, she must mention it to someone else. If these things are serious issues, it would be justifiable but because she is so sensitive, everything rubs her the wrong way. I am not the only Aries in my office. All of the Aries try to keep the conversations work related. My opinion may sound harsh but believe me, I don't dislike her. I am sure she sees my faults as clearly as I see hers. My goal with this Cancer is to minimize the negative and to focus on the work at hand. Anything else is unacceptable and dismissible. If something is wrong, I will look on the bright side. My optimism will repel her like her negativity repels me. If it's not about work, I don't want to know about it.

The other day she mentioned that she had to get therapy for her back. She had to get shots and needs to go twice a week. I listened to her talk about it for an hour at work. She sometimes has a limp. Often, she makes a lot of noises at her desk. One co-worker asked to switch cubicles to a location far from the Cancer. He was granted his request. From what I can tell, Cancers need attention and if they don't get it, they are unhappy. My approach with her, because I know she will annoy me, is to not indulge in long conversations. I am always busy. I don't allow her to chat me up for an hour at a time anymore. I don't ask her any personal questions. I know this seems cold but if I show any interest beyond the normal co-worker interest, she will take it to another level. I notice that other people in the office treat her this way but avoid her as well. I don't avoid her. I'm cordial and I try not to ask any personal questions.

Cancers need to find hobbies and things they like to do that will consume their time. That is a good thing for them because they need to focus their attention on something other than their relationships. If the Cancer doesn't have a hobby, you will be the hobby. Even though Cancers are nurturers, they don't tend to have a lot of children or any at all. I always find that weird somehow. They are caring, sensitive and nurturing but not very fond of children. They will have pets, maybe.

Cancers can be a downer for fun loving Aries. We don't have the energy to try to make them happy every minute of the day. We like people who are already happy. The weight of a Cancer friendship can be burdensome for us. A Cancer would have to have planets in their rising or moon that lifts the depressing energy. My whole life, I befriended one woman as a Cancer friend. She had planets in Aries, and she married an Aries man. She was a quiet person, hard worker and didn't complain. She had an illness, but she didn't like to talk about it. She got sick at work and had me call her husband. He came to the office and carried her to the car. I was impressed with the dynamic of their relationship. Other than that, her illness was never a topic of discussion.

We worked together for a company that didn't pay well. It was a source of aggravation for both of us. When I became a manager at another company, I told her we were hiring. The pay was substantially better. Of the earth signs, Cancer is cardinal and isn't hesitant to change and the money was the motivation. She applied at the company I was working for and we hired her. I didn't want to be her manager because I felt that would affect our friendship. When I left the company for an even better opportunity, she remained.

Cancers are reliable and loyal, but they require a lot of attention. I've never dated a Cancer man because I found them to be too dependent. For an Aries man, a Cancer woman may be just right for him. If you want a woman who will care for you and nurture you, get a Cancer. If you want someone who will care about your every whim, she's your girl. If you want a woman who appears to be weak and sick, so that you can be her knight in shining armor, you've found your wife. I've known this Cancer woman for over twenty years and she and her Aries husband are still married.

Cancers are excellent friends. They will help you no matter what is going on in their lives and their desire to help is genuine. They are always giving and helpful when they aren't focused on their own problems. Cancers center their lives around their personal relationships which is also a trait they share with Aries. The difference is that, Aries tend to cut off people after we outgrow them, and the Cancer will be cut off from people because people outgrow them. Even so, Cancers have plenty of associates.

The Cancer I work with believes that she is cheerful and positive. She tries hard, but everything has an undertone of gloom. She doesn't like when it's quiet or if people don't consult her first. She wants to know what everyone is doing and would like to oversee something. Unfortunately, she tends to like when people are negative, and she spends a lot of time talking about things that are negative. As an Aries, if something doesn't involve me, I don't want any part of it.

I have a relative who likes to start arguments. She has to mention every negative thing she can about something. Dating is not safe. Driving is dangerous.

Living in New York will get you killed. Men are strange. Yet, she has done every one of those things, but she will caution anyone else who dares to try because in her defense, she cares. She can keep her caring to herself as far as I'm concerned.

When she is upset, it is best not to be around her because she will start an argument about anything. Once, we argued about collard greens. She tried to say she was joking. There was no joke involved. She grabbed the plate out of my hand. I won't go into full details as I am not trying to anger myself over something that happened years ago. I stopped speaking to her for eight years. I'm still not looking forward to spending time around her because I don't like negative energy. I realize that she is older than me, so out of respect, I stay away because if I said what I wanted to say, it would hurt her tender feelings. I've hurt the feelings of Cancers before and I wasn't even trying, so imagine if I tried.

LEO

Leos! I know some good ones and a few bad ones. Even the bad ones are good in an Aries opinion. You can't have a relationship with every Leo you meet. Some of them are best as friends. Leos have confidence even when they don't know why. If ever a sign was a good match for an Aries, it is a Leo because they match our energy. The thing is you must find one who has self-esteem and positive energy. A Leo with negative energy is a complainer, abusive, an alcoholic, and a liar. You don't want to get around one of those. The good news is that there aren't that many. I only know a few bad ones.

Leos are lions so let them roar. Have you seen a lion strutting around? He knows he is the king. He is in charge and he is confident. He doesn't need your approval, but he likes it. Lions are gorgeous with their manes flowing around their heads. If you ever hear one roar, it's intimidating. Leos are like the lion because he is confident and regal. He has a plan and he will get it done. Leos are social and he will rally his group around his ideas. He knows who can help him and he will not hesitate to round the troops up.

The Leos keywords are I will. The Leo will, yes, he will. Whatever it is, it will get done if the Leo has anything to do with it. Leos are fire signs, so they bring a lot of energy with them. They are lively and their positivity is contagious. They are fixed signs which mean they are stubborn. Once they decide, it is solid. It is hard to get a Leo to change her mind. Even in the face of difficulty, Leos are survivors.

Alternatively, there are Leos who are negative, and they change the whole vibe in the room. They complain and argue about everything. If they believe something that is wrong, no matter what evidence you present, they will not believe a word you are saying. Their mind is made up. This Leo will argue with you about everything and he is always wrong. Nine times out of ten this Leo didn't graduate high school and has lived in a negative environment. He or she shouldn't lead anyone.

The best Leos are ones who have finished high school because they are forced to learn and to get different ideas from the ones they learned at home. The more education a Leo gets, the better. You don't want a Leo running around spreading bad information or rallying the troops to rob a bank. I am sure this type of Leo exists. I don't want to meet them.

Leos are too busy trying to be famous or special or the best at everything. Leos are independent and are always looking for ways to advance. They like money and the limelight. The worst thing about a Leo is that they are too much for some people. I find it entertaining. The bragging, boasting, and showing off doesn't bother me. I like confident people. What I don't like, is when the bragging and boasting becomes gossiping or downing someone that they find less important. That is rare but it does happen.

Most Leos like the underdog. They like people who are in trouble or who need help. They want to be a hero. I like heroes. Leos like to have fun and do things. You won't find a Leo in the house for long because they are always on the go.

I have a lot of Leo friends because we have a lot of things in common. If I say, "Let's go." They say, "When?" And vice versa. Leos like to be in control, so it is rare to find one that has a substance addiction. Also, if they are in the spotlight, they don't want to make a fool of themselves. Leos do not want to be made a fool of in public by anyone which is a trait shared by Aries.

Leos have a temper just like an Aries. Fire for fire. Whereas, just about anything will set off an Aries, the thing that will set off a Leo is if they see someone being mistreated.

The Aries will calm down faster than the Leo and sometimes, we look at the Leos anger and wonder why they are so angry. It really is amusing to us. It's like watching ourselves. I have spent a lot of time with Leos and their anger is rarely directed at an Aries. If there is ever an Aries and Leo argument, the Leo backs down. If the Leo doesn't back down, the Aries will end the relationship. Period. Remember, this is my experience as an Aries, and this has always been the situation with me and Leos. We can't have two leaders. If the Leo is leading in the Aries/Leo relationship, it's because the Aries allows the Leo to lead. We like to see someone else in charge but when it comes right down to it, we are running the show behind the scenes. We trust them and that says a lot because we don't trust easily.

Leos are a fixed sign which means they don't like change. Whatever ideas and beliefs they had years ago, they will stick to it. They tend to like certain people and it is hard to get into to their group of friends. They make judgements about people and tend to stick to those ideas. You must persuade a Leo to try new things. This can be a hard task. Even if they try it, they still won't like it. If the Leo wants to impress you, he or she will do it with minimal complaints.

My Leo girlfriends are like myself, but we are different when it comes to relationships with men. I like to be married and my girlfriends like relationships, but they are not focused on marriage. They want to be married but if it doesn't happen then it doesn't. I, on the other hand, will make it happen.

My Leo friends go out by themselves, eat by themselves, and spend a lot of time chatting with men. My Leo friends know what they are looking for in a man. They have the same requirements that they had years ago, my requirements have changed. I am more willing to date men from other nationalities. My friends' tastes are more specific. I have always dated and married men who were different from me. Leos are outgoing but they will not embrace a partner who is different. I had a conversation with a Leo friend who has been divorced for twenty years.

"Mel, you are going to marry an Egyptian?"
"Yes. I like him. We have a lot in common and I like the fact that he doesn't talk much."

"He doesn't know English," says Leo.
"Very little," I laugh. "I am going to visit him a few times before I make my decision."
"By yourself?"
"I travel by myself all the time. Besides, I have talked to him on the phone often. He's a nice guy. A very stable Taurus."
"I would never date a man that isn't black and American."

I had another conversation with my Leo friend about ten years ago after I married my Puerto Rican ex-husband.

"I met a guy when I went on a work trip," says Leo.
"I thought you were using a dating sight. Is he from the dating sight?" I asked.
"No, he was a white guy at the bar at the hotel I was staying at," she said. "I'm going to try to date outside my race."
I was in shock. Had I influenced her to go outside of her boundaries? "No way! When are you going to see him again?"
"I'm thinking about it," said the Leo.

Did she? No. That is one Leo friend, but I have another one who is white, and she is the same way. Before I got married to my first husband (Taurus of nine years), the Leo and I went out and she was trying to set me up with different guys at the club. She introduced me to every black guy she saw. I asked her why she didn't talk to them since she seemed to have a friendly repour with them, she said, "I never thought about it. I've dated women but I never dated outside my race." When an Arab guy asked me to dance (the Gemini) she was shocked.

I'm not saying my friends are racist, but they are only comfortable dating men (or women) they are familiar with and who are the same race as them. Of the Aries people that I know, I am not the only one who dates outside of my race. This may not be specific to a sign and more of a person's environment. My sons' father is like the other Leos I know, he has mainly dated black women, but my son is a Leo who dates outside of his race.

I know plenty of Leos who have been my best friends. They have shared their dating experiences and friendships with me. You would think that our relationship would be competitive. I never felt competitive with Leo females, but I felt the men were competing with me. Looking back on it, the men who were competitive wanted to feel more accomplished than I and it would have been better if they were already more accomplished before they met me.

The female Leos were similar to me. We are high achievers. We buy homes, have good jobs, travel, and are alphas. We don't compete with each other, we uplift each other. We spend a lot of time talking about how we manage our busy lives and we respect the different ways we do things. We talk about how being an alpha is problematic and wonder how easy it would be if we were submissive. Personally, I wouldn't mind being submissive if I found someone that I could trust, who was actively managing his life, and who didn't need my help to get himself together.

To be honest, only low vibrating or negative energy Leo men compete with me. The higher vibes and positive energy Leo men nurture and encourage my successes. If I am friends with the male Leo then, I get the encouragement. And Leos are generous. They like to show off so that comes with spending money and wining and dining. I imagine a poor Leo would be uncomfortable in his skin or in a lot of debt unless he has a more fugal sign in his birth chart holding him back from over spending.

Leos like compliments. The more you compliment them, the happier they are. It is easy for us because there is a lot that we like about high vibrating Leos. Leos are givers like us. They will buy you the world. They like wine and food. If you want to know what the sex is like, well, it's great. A Leo that doesn't over indulge in alcohol and drugs has the stamina to match our high energy. I love to give compliments when they are deserved, and Leos deserve it.

A Leo man will defend your honor. They don't want anyone messing with their women. They like a show, too. I dated a Leo in high school who would go everywhere with me. We were in the mall and two guys bumped into me without saying excuse me. The Leo backed one of the guys up against the wall and made both apologize to me. I was shocked but it was a turn on. Leos have rescued me more than I can count, and I wasn't expecting it because I am used to defending myself.

Even the Leos who aren't considered "bad boys" get into trouble. It's usually justified but their loud mouths attract it. They are real men so expect manly behavior. Can you tell I like them? I do but not those ignorant ones. The ones who argue with women, pick on people, and who can't keep a legal job. I avoid them.

Leos don't do well in school. They would rather do something else. If a Leo makes it out of high school and goes to college, it's because they know in order to achieve the goals they are aiming for, they will have to finish college. A smart Leo knows the value of education and if he can concentrate, he will find that he is smart enough to graduate. Leos must keep up with the Joneses. If their friends received further education, they will. Leos need to have positive influences in their lives to reach the height of achievement. If their influences are low achievers that is what they will imitate and strive for.

The Leos I know like surprises and birthday parties. I don't like either, but Leos are infectious. You will start to like what they like. Some are loud and obnoxious, but you will like it. The fun is contagious. Leos have a large appetite for everything and that includes sex. Leos live Utopian lives because they like to be happy. They find pleasure in most things. Leos are carefree but they are responsible and family oriented. They take care of their families which includes their mothers, wives, sons, daughters, brothers, cousins, nephews, nieces, fathers, and sisters.

VIRGO

I have had nice superficial conversations with Virgo women. We have lovely conversations, but Virgos are not my cup of tea. I wish I could put my finger on it, but I think it is because they are so critical and precise about everything. I don't have time for it. If I wanted to spend a whole day saying the correct word to describe a thing or to do something exactly how the manual says so, I wouldn't do it myself, I would get a Virgo to do it. I should have had a Virgo edit this guide for clarity and precision, but I can't wait for a Virgo to change it a million times and rearrange it because it isn't perfect.

For example, if I say, "Look at the dog." A Virgo will say, "That's a puppy." If I say, "Where did the girl go?" Virgo will say, "She's a teenager." This is how all our conversations go. I have had a lot of conversations with them and it isn't worth mentioning. Virgos should work on letting trivial things go then, they wouldn't have to always apologize to people for being an asshole. Virgos seem angry to me, like, anger is always simmering underneath their quiet exterior. Unjustified anger. They imagine that people don't like them, but I don't think anyone is thinking about them at all. Maybe that is why so many of them become murderers.

To be honest, I upset them. I could care less about what they are doing but the ones I have worked with or grew up with or my relatives, seem to have a problem with me. Imagine that! I don't know why, and I don't care to know. I'm sure they would tell me if I asked. I'm sure they have told other people because Virgos don't mind spreading gossip. Gossip is their thing.

The Virgo symbol is the Virgin. What is that supposed to mean? I guess it's their innocence. They seem innocent. They behave like they don't know what's going on, on a regular basis. They know. They pretend not to know. Everything is brand new to them, but it isn't.

The keywords for Virgos are I analyze. They analyze everything. It is a critical analysis. Nothing is good enough. Virgos are mutable which means their ideas change. They change their thinking and ideas because they want the best and the most perfect version.

Sad news, nothing is perfect and so, Virgos are always irritated about everything. They are wrapped too tight for me. Loosen up. No one cares about the small details as much as an over analyzing Virgo. Their level of frustration is probably high all day, every day.

Virgos try too hard to be cute and demure and it irritates me. I wouldn't spend my spare time hanging with any. They seem nice enough in the beginning, but they are your secret haters Aries. Believe what I tell you. Heed my warning. If another sign is giving you a hard time, my bet is that they have Virgo in their birth chart.

I manage to keep it civil in the work place when I work with them. I try not to do projects with them. As long as we have a surface relationship, everything is fine. When I manage a Virgo, they are never happy about anything.

The Virgos in my family think everyone is their servant. I don't know where this mentality came from, but it has caused plenty of strife in my family dynamics. This is going to be a short section because I steer clear of Virgos as much as I can to keep them from crying about some imaginary offense I have done when I know all I did was breath.

One other thing I notice about Virgos, they are very homely and frumpy. I only know one who looks like a movie star when she gets dressed up. That woman might have Libra somewhere in here birth chart. I don't care if they are wearing Versace or some hot item from Paris, it looks like a potato shack if a Virgo puts it on. I don't know how they do that to clothes, but they do. Either they don't care what they look like in public or they don't know what looks good on them. Or maybe they try too hard to look good and it never goes as planned.

The most comfortable Virgo is a naked Virgo. They are comfortable not being weighed down by clothes. I imagine they attend nudist beaches. Don't ask me how I know this information, but it came from the lips of a Libra who witnessed the shameless display. I wish I didn't know, to be honest. Even if they don't like their bodies, they are comfortable being naked. Maybe that's where the Virgin symbolism comes from. You know the newness of birth and being virgin like a baby, I'm guessing. Then again, Libras lie, and this may not be true at all.

I hear that Virgo men are smart but they like gossip and thrive off of it. Virgos are opinionated and judgmental. They seem similar to us but don't let this suck you in. The things that make them different are their hate and negativity and it will cause you endless discomfort. For example, I received an email from a Virgo on social media whom I had never met in my life. Let me say this, he was insulting to the point where I was like this is sexual harassment.

I deleted the conversation and didn't say a word. He texted me back. "Hey, don't you want to talk? What's your phone number?" I blocked him. Worst Virgo ever. I don't know if he was joking or if he thought I like to be insulted. He couldn't handle my confidence on social media, and he had never met me a day in his life. I get visceral reactions from Virgos.

A Virgo is only compatible with another Virgo. And for God's sake, a Virgo should have Virgo children. No one is good enough for a Virgo unless it's another Virgo. If an Aries doesn't have Virgo in his or her chart, stay away because they will crush your soul with all of the mind-numbing minutia, negative nothingness, and the seething under surface hate.

Avoid them.

LIBRA

If I had years to discuss Libras, I would. I lived with one most of my life. The men are attracted to me and have tricked (yes, tricked) me into thinking they were stable. A stable balanced Libra is a myth. I have never met one.

Libras are wonderful people as friends. They can out talk us, and they know about all kinds of interesting things. They know good jokes and are great story tellers. Libras, like Gemini, are party people. Where is the party? At the Libras house. Libras like nice things. They always want the latest stuff but, who's buying the stuff? I don't know any Libras who buy their own stuff. Some man or woman is buying stuff for them, believe that! Libras are the mistress of some sugar daddy or the boy toy of some sugar momma. They like to be taken care of by someone. If you like to take care of someone, the Libra is for you.

Libras spend their money on food and clothes. I don't know one Libra who knows how to save their own money. And selfish, you haven't met selfish until you've met a Libra. Libra is always handing out money but guess what, they don't like it. They do it because it makes them look good and that is why they make sure everyone knows they are doing it. Aries are secret givers and that is how it should be. We give in ways people aren't even aware of because we like it. Libras want you to know but deep down, they resent having to give money to people.

Libras are like Leos because they like to be noticed. They are consumed by what people think of them. Aries don't care what people think of them and people naturally notice us without us having to do anything. Libras are different from us in all kinds of ways.

If you think Aries take astrology seriously, you don't know any Libras. All day with the scales. "We are balanced. We are justice." I think they and everyone in the world is not looking at that correctly. A good Libra would be a balanced Libra and Libras should strive to be balanced. They weren't born balanced. If anything, they were born with one of those scales touching the ground. All signs must find what makes them great and Libras must achieve balance. So many Libras out here talking about being balanced and can't pay their bills because they went and got their hair done. Libras love their hair! A Libra would rather get their hair done than eat.

Libras can be superficial; only caring about how a person looks. Libras are not at the height of fashion themselves. Sure, they know how to dress to impress but no one is dressed to impress every day, not even them.

I have a lot of anger towards Libras so you might want to skip this section.

Most mothers love their children and if they have a favorite, they don't say it out loud. Libra mothers always have a favorite and it's no secret. Usually, they have horrible relationships with their daughters because of the struggle of young versus old. Libras tend to be attractive and they want to be the prettiest woman in the room. Jealousy toward a daughter is common. Hopefully, the Libras chart will have some other signs to combat these awful Libra characteristics, but I have not met any.

When I asked my friends about their mothers, can you guess what the link between us was? Our mothers were all Libras. We had horror stories we would tell. Not one of us was laughing or joking. Sure, it made us strong and independent, but it would have been nice to have someone who listened to us and gave us some good advice. A mother who wasn't wrapped up in her make-up or the way she dressed, would have been nice. On the flip side, when she wasn't concerned about how she looked, she wasn't concerned about anything. She is a lazy homemaker, the Libra woman. They live their lives trying to impress people because they care too much about what other people think but in honesty, they are unkempt. Show up at their house when they aren't expecting you, I dare you.

Libra females are fun to hang out with because they are always cooking. I'm not saying they know how to cook but some of them do and some of them don't. The ones that cook well should be chefs but once the lazy sets in, forget about it. A Libra has to be in the mood to do things otherwise, it won't turn out well. They push themselves to do things because they don't want people to talk bad about them. It would be better if they took a note from the Aries play book and said no for a change. Libras don't know how to say no.

And.The.Libra.Men! Can we say hot mess? They don't know whether they like you or not. They don't know if they are coming or going, but if something goes wrong, you can best believe it is your fault. They have a reputation, you know, of being perfect. They have never done any wrong, ever.

If you ever meet a Libra man who says, "I don't like know-it-alls." Run! He is the know-it-all. He won't listen to a word you say. He will start things and never finish. You will think he is like you but under that niceness is a wishy-washy negative person, unless you get lucky and find a balanced one. I never met one.

When a man says he can love two women at a time, he's probably a Libra. He thinks he loves two women. He's really not sure and may not love anyone because they fall out of whatever it is, fast. Leos hate being alone, but Libras hate it more. If you are with one now, he's probably juggling six women; unless, of course, you have one of those balanced ones, a unicorn.

People say opposites attract and therefore, Libras are our opposite. We have something they want, and we want something they have. I get it. My mother is a Libra and I married one, so I know what I am talking about.

Libras say they like romance, but they are not romantic. Libras will fight in a gang, but they do not have your back if it's just you and them. You will have to fend for yourself. For example, I was accosted by a homeless person and my Libra husband sat in the car and watched. He acted like he didn't even see it. Cowards.

The thing that really makes me angry about Libra men is that they pretend they don't like sex. They want you to believe they are prudes. Why? You have plenty of women that you are having sex with, but you can't admit that you like having sex? Then, why do it? It is the dumbest thing I have noticed about them. It's one thing if you don't care about sex and are looking for a long-term relationship but when you are running around with a whole gaggle of women having sex, don't come at me talking about, "I don't even like sex." I kid you not. Many Libra men have said this, and I can only wonder why this is something to say. I think they believe this makes them seem like less of a dog because they know they are dogs.

I had one say, "I know I am a good man." Alert! Good men don't make that announcement, ever. It's a "doing" thing, not a "saying" thing. You don't have to say it if you know you are doing things that good men do.

Libras are contrary and that is something many Aries can't stand. Stand by your words, say what you mean, and mean what you say. I'm not trying to be extra mean, but I don't think Libras should have children. Men or women. They are too selfish. The Libra man I knew spent very little time with his son. It was like he had no idea what to do with a kid. He did things he liked, and the kid clearly didn't like doing those things. It is like they are not in touch with their inner child. Libras have no idea what it's like to be a kid and I don't know why that is. Even when they are doing fun stuff, they do it in an adult manner. It's like they hold themselves back. Maybe they don't know how to truly have fun and they like us because we do. Maybe they are always pretending, and we are never pretending. Whatever it is, I don't like it.

They gossip but they are more of a lying gossiper. They will make up what they believe happened and it never happened. It is part of their being good at telling stories and jokes, but it isn't funny when it comes to other people's lives. They get along well with Virgos because they both like lies and gossip. The bigger the better with them. I've witnessed Virgos and Libras in my family make up whole lies, from a minor rumor, that would set your hair on fire. The Virgo will throw something out there, a small spark, and the Libra will take it and spread it like a forest fire.

I would like to advise you stay away from Libras, but I know you won't. Enjoy it while it lasts, and I hope for your sake you found one of those balanced ones. Their goal in life should be to find balance, otherwise, they can potentially ruin a lot of lives. Libras come in contact with a lot of people and a low vibrating one will have a lot of relationships before settling down. Their callous behavior is hard to imagine when you have only seen the happy go lucky Libra. They hide it well, but it is there. Aries men do well with Libra women. They are more successful with Libras than an Aries woman with a Libra man. I think this is because Libra men are too feminine for us. It would be nice if those qualities balanced with our ability to be masculine, but it doesn't if the two people aren't compatible. This is why the femininity of the Libra woman and the over masculinity of the Aries male works better.

I don't need a man nagging me and complaining. I don't nag and complain. I hate it. As a woman, those are things I find detestable in other women and it sends me over the edge in a man. I found myself telling the Libra to "man up" because he complained about everything. I can nag myself to death so, what do I need him for? It was a constant battle to do housework. He wanted to wash clothes and cook which is fine if you are going to do it. I don't need you to ask me or tell me. I think he was just saying it so that I would know that those are things he is capable of doing but he never actually did them. Maybe he wanted me to ask him to do it? I don't know. I like a man to do things without having to say anything. As a matter of fact, I like doing things around the house. I would rather a man do things I hate doing, like things with the car or in the yard. Mind you, these were not arguments that we had. No, these were the things that made us different. The unsaid things that can wear a relationship out. I needed a more manly man and he needed a more manly woman.

Libras tend to collect friends frequently. They change best friends a lot. They also end friendships quickly. A Libra will have a best one day out of the blue and then a week later, no longer talk to the person. The people they call their friends are not really friends. They are associates but ok. When the falling out occurs, it is always the other person's fault because a Libra can do no wrong. I have never known a Libra to take responsibility for their actions in my forty-nine years of life.

Libras are cardinal signs which means, like us, they start a lot of things but rarely finish them. They don't have the ability to make decisions which causes them to always be late and not be able to focus. They don't want to make the wrong decision. This is one of the reasons why they have so many relationships. They are never sure who is the right person for them. They will start a new relationship without leaving the old one. They are similar to Geminis in this respect and the two signs get along very well.

The keywords for Libras are I balance. The only way this is true is that I have seen Libras take the side of the loser in an argument. The Libra will defend the loser and add their two cents. They like a debate. They see all sides of an argument because they aren't sure who they agree with so that is a plus. Like air, Libras are in everyone's business.

I work with a Libra and I noticed something. They spend more time talking than working. Libras are friendly and social. They always have a story to share. They like joking more than working. Libras manage to keep their jobs because people like them and they are attractive. They don't like to be disliked. They tend to get promotions because they know how to make themselves look good.

SCORPIO

Scorpio women can keep a secret and they will use their sexuality to go far in life. They are very reserved and quiet. They are watching you. If they have something to say, they will say it, and they don't care about your response. A Scorpio woman's sex life is private. If you hear about it, it's because she is secure in her relationship. The man is the one. Otherwise, she will not talk about her relationship unless you are a close friend and even then, she will not get too deep.

Scorpio women are always watching their backs. They don't trust you. They will think bad of you before they think good of you. Everyone is up to something or out to get them. Their female friends are usually family members and she is watching them around her man. She's good at analyzing a situation. She knows if you want to fight or if you're just talking.

She will protect her man and the man she is looking for has to keep her secrets. I have a relative who is a Scorpio and she never got married. She is a sad sort. She never found the one and she refuses to accept anything less. She drinks too much and smokes too much. She has male friends but at her age, 72, she will die doing what she does. I refuse to give up.

This woman keeps her nails done and her hair. She wears sophisticated clothes. She never wore sneakers or jeans. She has been a classy woman her whole life. What she does in the dark is her business.

I know a lot of Scorpio women who were strippers or who are in the sex industry. They took the money from that and worked magic. They became real estate owners, business owners, and millionaires. I get along better with older Scorpio women who have mellowed into their age. They appreciate my honesty. I value their honesty and they have great business advice.

The keywords for Scorpios are I desire. They desire a lot of things, but love predominates their lives. The Scorpio man desires someone like him. This will be hard to find because he is unique. He is a rare bird. They go through a lot of women or men because they are searching. They aren't doing it solely because they like sex. Oh no. Scorpios are fixed which means they are stable and secure. They want stability and security. Believe it or not, love doesn't come easy for them because they don't communicate well. They live in secrets and silence. They expect you to read their minds.

When Scorpios aren't thinking about death, they are thinking about why things die. Why is life so difficult? Why can't everyone just do what they are supposed to do and push on? Why does everything have to be so negative? I don't know but if anyone can figure out the answer, it's a Scorpio.

Scorpios are scorpions. Why are they like scorpions? Scorpions are predators, scorpions have a long mating ritual, and scorpion venom is valuable. Why do these traits resemble the Scorpio? Have you ever dated a Scorpio? If so, you would know. They saw you before you saw them. They watch the people they are interested in. When they finally make contact, if they are looking for more than sex, the process of getting to know you takes time. They are not rushing into it, but they will be consistent. You have to be patient with a Scorpio. If you get put off by their slow actions, then you've missed out because chances are, he is trying to get to know you and not just ravish your body.

Why is the venom valuable? For the most part, Scorpios are honest and the truth hurts. With their moodiness, the venom can spill out. Whatever it is they are criticizing, it's probably something you should work on. They will tell you about yourself because they have been observing you. An example of this venom reminds me of a situation in my office. I had a Scorpio boss who paid attention to everything even when you didn't think he did. A co-worker asked me if I was pregnant once because I was sick one morning and throwing up. I thought that was a rude question, but she is an Aries and we say whatever we feel. A day later, the Aries co-worker was sick, and the Scorpio supervisor asked her if she was pregnant and he looked at me and winked. My co-worker immediately understood what he was getting at and was a bit embarrassed for assuming that I was pregnant the day before.

I have had three Scorpio supervisors and as employers go, I like working for Scorpios. They recognize my experience and acknowledge my intelligence. They allow me to work quietly and on my own. They don't micromanage me, but they will come over to check on me. One of my supervisors said he reminds himself to check on me to make sure I am still alive because I am quiet. They always take time out of their day to tell me they appreciate me. I like it but they may be somewhat attracted to me. It seems to be the same behavior I get when I meet a Scorpio outside of work. The attraction is undeniable.

There is always some guy standing back watching me. When I am alone, he will come up and introduce himself. This guy is a Scorpio. He doesn't care if I have a boyfriend and I do. He will continue to watch me and when I break up with my boyfriend, who is probably a Leo, the Scorpio swoops in. Not right away though and best believe he wasn't really waiting. He was seeing girls the whole time and still seeing them when he approaches again after I break up with the Leo. He will test me to see what kind of person I am. Soon he won't know if he is testing me or if I am testing him.

I don't care who the Scorpio is seeing or talking to or dating because he wants to date me. If he waited for me to break up with my boyfriend, then I know he likes me more than he is letting on. I appear not to care either way, but he is in my thoughts. They are attracted to my cool demeanor.

I'm not going to be too eager because I know his reputation. He has lots of girls and they are pretty. You think the Scorpio man picks his women based on looks but that is not true. Unlike the Libra, the Gemini, or the Leo, the Scorpio man wants one woman and he knows this at a young age. He likes sex and he isn't ashamed to say it but that is not how he picks his woman. Sex is sex. His woman has to have a lot more going on than sex.

Aries women have Scorpio men wondering. Why isn't she falling all over me? Why won't she do what I say? Who is this woman who is catching what I'm throwing? She is calling me out of my normal behavior. If you have no patience, you won't notice these things about the Scorpio. Some of you think Scorpios are corny because they are always watching somebody like a stalker. He seems creepy. I appreciate someone who studies his victim, I mean, his next conquest.

Aries finds the quiet mysterious sexy Scorpio man very appealing and he is smart as hell. His calm is good for us because he does not jump to conclusions. He wants to know the full story. He will mull it over. He talks when he wants to and then, he won't. Like Aries, he needs down time. He can be depressing if he has too many planets in water signs. He can easily get addicted to drugs or alcohol. He is a deep thinker, but he won't tell you what he's thinking. Of all the people he trusts, he can trust an Aries and if she is patient enough, he will tell her more than he tells anyone. This relationship works better when both have signs in Aries and Scorpio in their birth chart.

Scorpios are known to be very sexual and they do have a lot of sex, but they are patient when you tell them you are not interested in having sex. I have dated guys who dropped me like a hot potato when they realized I was not interested in having sex. I'm sure they were seeing other people as well. Not the Scorpio. He wanted to know what I was about so even though the possibility of getting sex was slim, he was curious enough to try to get to know me. He didn't harass me like the Capricorn asking me who was I seeing on the side. He didn't run off like the Aquarius who didn't want a relationship in the first place. Scorpios are looking for the one and if he is, not giving him sex is probably a good thing. It doesn't mean he will stop having sex with the other girls he calls for sex. You know, he has girls on call. If he's not looking for the one, he will chat with you and be your friend. He will see those other girls and won't take it personal. If he believes you are the one, he will drop those other girls and you will know that he isn't interested in anyone else but you.

If he cuts those other chicks off then, you have a keeper. If he has sex with you and them, then you are just another one of them. Don't be one of the groupies, it's not a good look. Scorpios don't talk much in relationships unless he has a lot of air signs in his birth chart, so watch what he does. The problem with most Aries women is that we don't have the patience for Scorpios or Capricorns because they take a relationship slow and aren't very talkative. They will show you how they feel. We have to pay attention and a lot of us won't. We go for the loud mouth Leo, Gemini or Libra. We like fun people who probably aren't ready to settle down. Aries like to have fun, but we like to be in a relationship, too.

I was talking to a Scorpio friend on the phone and his take on relationships was interesting.

"I smoke weed because relationships require too much thought," he said.
"What?"
"I have to consider her feelings and what I need to do to make her happy and how I'm living my life. Am I doing me or am I doing me because of her?" Says the Scorpio.
"If you're not compatible then, you shouldn't be in the relationship. If you are compatible, it should work out."
"No one is compatible with me," said the Scorpio. "I have dated millions of women. Nothing."
"Is it possible you are leading with your dick and not having conversations? If you are high most of the time, how will you know if you have anything in common?"
"She should like to get high but that can't be the only thing she likes to do," he replied.
"If she gets high as much as you do, would you want to have a relationship with her?" I asked.

"There is no way I can be with a woman who gets as high as I do. I would stop smoking if my woman smoked more than me," he stated.

"If you don't talk to them and you are dating them because they like to smoke, how do you plan to find the woman of your dreams? You will have to smoke less and talk more," I added.

"Yea, I'm going to die alone," he said.

In hindsight, the Scorpio was probably interested in me more than I knew. I was oblivious because he never said he was interested in me. Yet, we hung out a lot and he called me, but I assumed he was talking to other women. He never asked me to be his girlfriend. Then, I moved away, and we lost touch.

I'm sharing this conversation because it is funny, and it has nothing to do with anything except how Scorpios think.

"Once, I got so high, I could read a dude's mind. He wanted to have sex with me. I could tell by the way he was looking at me," said the Scorpio.

"Were the guy's lips moving?"

"No, but I heard him loud and clear with my mind."

"Did you have sex with him?" I asked.

"No, the high wore off thank God, but I thought about it," he said seriously.

If you think Aries are in their head, so are Scorpios and the things they think about are different. What makes the relationship work is the honesty. I am honest to a fault and when a Scorpio feels like telling you something, it's honest. I'm sure there are some low vibrating liars out there, but I haven't come across them. I'm a bit judgmental but I have never judged the Scorpio man for anything he has said or done.

When a Scorpio gets moody, I ignore them but not for too long because they hate that. There is almost a formula or method to it, and you won't know it unless you care. If you don't care, the relationship won't last a hot second. It's easy for us to forgive them when they get moody because for the most part, they are always giving us attention. I might act like I don't like attention, but from the right person, it is fabulous. And the way to get it has to be right. You can't just rush up on me. My man has to be sly with it. Turn on the fireplace and fix me a glass of wine, order dinner, take off my clothes… I don't have to tell a Scorpio anything. He's not just sex, he has romance, too.

Scorpios are good in relationships. I don't know where the rumor about them being bachelors came from, but I know a lot of them that are in long term relationships. The bachelors that I know are Geminis. Scorpios may take longer to find someone but like I mentioned, they are looking for the one. They are good providers if they don't let any of their bad habits like (drinking, partying, and smoking weed) get the best of them. They usually know what they want to do in life and somehow manage to do it. Perseverance, they have that. I met a lot of Scorpios in college. Education is important to them.

I like them because they are calm when we are acting off the chain or wilding out. They are observing everything. We give them something to consider. Scorpios will consider us harmless and a nice shiny project. They will see the fun side and wonder about us. They know we have a temper but that is something that fascinates them. We are very similar to them and sometimes, this is a turn off. Also, if they feel that you have harmed them, they will cut you off forever.

An example of their calm reaction to intense situations is when I was driving with a Scorpio while it was raining and like I normally do, I was speeding. The Scorpio had ridden with me before and my speed never bothered him. Other signs would sit on the edge of the seat. I make Pisces nervous, Tauruses have grabbed the steering wheel almost killing us all, and Leos have argued with me the whole ride. I was impressed with the Scorpio's confidence in my driving in the rain. He didn't even ask me to slow down. So, when I hit the puddle and started to skid into a field headed directly for a huge oak tree, he didn't utter a word. He opened his mouth soundlessly. He watched me as I handled the steering wheel, but he said nothing.

The car careened onto the grass as I managed to maneuver the wheel and direct the tires out of the spinout. We stopped right in front of the tree. It was a driving miracle. The Scorpio looked at me and said, "Who are you? Maria Andretti?" We sat there for a few seconds, laughing. We were not high or drunk. If so, it would have been a tragedy.

I turned the car around and got back on the road. I was a little more careful, but I was glad he didn't lose his shit. We were both shook up, but he didn't make it worse by grabbing the wheel or shouting. I was grateful for that. He let me concentrate on not getting us killed. He didn't blame me or tell me I shouldn't have been driving so fast.

As long as Scorpios keep their negative thoughts to a minimum, we can have a wonderful relationship. If the Scorpio is wondering what you are doing, that's less time wondering about the galaxy and where all the dead souls go. Talking to an Aries about some of those deep concerns is fascinating but if you keep things on the bright side, it would be better for both of you. A Scorpio will take negativity too far and if you are not in control of your own feelings, you will get wiped out by this emotional tidal wave. And yet, the best thing about a Scorpio is how deep they can get and that includes love. Scorpios want to be in love like Aries wants to be in love. Scorpio is looking for a love that is unconditional and Aries is looking for a love that lasts forever. We both want someone who is committed to the long term.

When I dated a Scorpio, I noticed that we had a weird habit of talking to each other with eye contact. We were so in tune to each other that we didn't have to say anything. A look could mean, "I'm ready to go." A look could mean, "Did you hear what he said?" We had our own secret language. Unfortunately, I can't be friends with a Scorpio man and have a relationship with another sign. The connection I have with Scorpios make other signs jealous and it seems to become all about me and the Scorpio. We have inside jokes that rub people the wrong way.

SAGITTARIUS

I have Sagittarius relatives. They know about everything. They are natural philosophers. Of the fire signs, they use their fire to throw themselves into a cause that they will be dedicated to their whole lives. I have seen them argue fiercely about their cause. They know it better than anyone because they have read on it and researched it for years. Sagittarius know what they are talking about. They know facts.

Sagittarius women get on my nerves. They try too hard to be my friend, and they seem like bullies to me. I don't like any of their jokes especially, when they try to make jokes about me. How dare you? They have no chill. They will try to take your man. I don't care how ugly they are, their confidence in stealing men is unreal.

If you don't like being teased, then I suggest you don't hang with Sagittarius women because they will try to hurt your feelings. Aries women have to fight them to assert our dominance. I don't suggest lowering your standards to their foolishness. The best thing to do is to ignore them. It does more damage.

Sagittarius key words are I understand because they understand everything. They read a lot. Sagittarius is the archer or centaur. What does this mean? The archer is good at hitting his target. The centaur is a beast who is half man half horse. A Sagittarius can use brains to get out of a difficult situation or run from it. A Sagittarius is not fighting unless it is absolutely necessary, and they are strong as a horse.

I remember my brother getting into an altercation once. A guy walked into him aggressively at the Burger King in Hempstead, New York when we were younger. My brother didn't say a word. He shoved the guy so hard he fell back, and I looked at the guy like a pit bull ready to snap. Altercation over but I was surprised at my little brother's strength. I don't remember any words being exchanged but I wouldn't call it a fight. It was over as quickly as it had started. I didn't have to do anything. As for being a beast, I have witnessed Sagittarius having crazy strength.

When my brother was eight, the jack that my father was using to lift the car so he could change a flat tire fell on him. My brother lifted the car so my father could slide from under the weight of the car. Is this true? I don't know. I wasn't there but a Libra told me, and we know how Libras lie. Seriously, Sagittarius have incredible strength.

I was talking to my Sagittarius brother about bowel movements. So, I say, "you should have one every time you eat. Food gets digested and it comes out. If you aren't taking a shit at least three times a day, you probably should see a doctor."
"There are people who don't have bowel movements three times a day," says Sagittarius.
"I'm sure there are but if you are eating three full meals a day, you should take a shit. Period."

"There are monks that don't shit three times a day. They eat one meal," he says.
"They should take one shit."
"There are people who fast. They don't have bowel movements at all."
"They shouldn't. Anyone else eating breakfast, lunch and dinner should take a shit or that person is going to have serious bowel problems in the future."
"You should start fasting," he mentions.
"I have days where I drink liquids. I have days where I don't eat meat. I cleanse."

My conversations are always about something random with them. We talk Aliens, UFO's, and things that most people don't think about. The other Sagittarius I know, is religious. He is borderline Jesus. He knows everything about our Lord and Savior. He even went to school to study theology. What he doesn't know is a forty-hour work week. Or work. Sagittarius have a lot of time to read and study even when they are not attending school. They would rather read than work or attend college. I know a lot of Sagittarius men who do not work forty-hour jobs. They try but it doesn't seem to be inherent to their nature unless they have a lot of earth signs in their birth chart.

The Sagittarius is mutable and restless. His mind needs to be active or he will be dull. Sagittarius are like Geminis, they move around a lot. They have a lot of friends and a lot of hobbies. When you talk to them, they tend to move from topic to topic but not as quickly as Gemini.

The Sagittarius girls seem to have a lot of fire. I worked with one and she was always busy and always hustling. She seemed a bit mannish as well. She hung out with a lot of the guys and she liked to party and have fun. I got along with her ok, but she said something to me that set me off. My normal is to fight but, I was at work, so I reported her. I have an issue with people who are unprofessional at work. If this had been a one and done, I would have over looked it but there were too many incidents of inappropriate work behavior. Maybe letting it slide the first few times when it was with other employees was why she thought she could do me the same way. I draw the line on disrespect. If we had been on the street, we would have been fighting.

Before the incident, she would ask me what I would do in certain work situations and I tried my best to give her some managerial tips. Like, you should NOT yell at an employee in front of other employees when they make a mistake. You take the person to your office and you have a sit-down conversation. You tell them how they made a mistake, how to correct the mistake, and give him or her a warning. If they repeat the mistake, give them a different role, offer training, or demotion. If they continue to make mistakes, termination.

I sent her to managerial training classes. She wasn't happy to go and skipped a few. Her co-worker, another manager, the Virgo wasn't excited either, but she went. I don't know why some people don't like learning new things if it will help to make them a better person or boost their career, but I don't think that has anything to do with a person's sign. Personally, I will go to any class you send me to if it is free and it means I will get a raise for gaining a new skill.

Sagittarius are sensitive people and wear their woes on their sleeve. They seem saddened by the world to me. They talk a lot about the world and the things that happen, things that need to change. Their focus is wide whereas an Aries focus is narrow. The Sagittarius mind is pulled in many different directions. They are very intelligent, but they do not live their lives on personal best.

They want the best for everyone. They are generous to a fault. They are selfless. So, in that respect, a Sagittarius is a good friend to have and they have a lot of friends. More friends than any other sign. Real friends. People who will house them and feed them. People who will drive them to work and give them the shirt off their backs. Why? Because a Sagittarius would do the same for their friends.

When I think of the Sagittarius, they really are like prophets or philosophers. They are not motivated by what most people are motivated by. They don't really care for regular jobs. They are not motivated by money. They view the world and they judge it. If they could go around talking to people about the books they read or the YouTube video they saw on aliens, or the effects of social media on the human mind, or homelessness, they would. They don't care about your regular life or your job. They want to talk about the mysteries of the world.

Even the wealthy and successful Sagittarius doesn't care much for fame or wealth. It was a means to an end. Sagittarius are creative. They can play instruments, write poems, and draw. They spend their time being creative.

They make their money from their creative endeavors and humanitarian adventures. A Sagittarius is more of a self-sacrificing person. They give to people and never complain about having anything. That's probably why people tend to go out of their way to do things for them.

I remember once I overheard a conversation between the Virgo and the Sagittarius while in the office. I mean, they were standing right in front of me. The Virgo asked the Sagittarius if she planned to move once she got her raise. The Sagittarius lived in the hood. No disrespect but this was common knowledge. She talked about the events of her neighborhood and they were hair raising. The Virgo who made the same amount of money, lived in a better neighborhood and wanted her friend to live the way she was living. The Sagittarius was not impressed she said, and I quote, "Nope. I like my neighborhood."

The Virgo said, "I don't know how you live there with the burglaries, the shootouts and the noise."

The Sagittarius replied, "I've lived there for a long time. I know everyone. It doesn't bother me. Besides, if I stay there, I will have more money to feed my kids."

The Sagittarius was also giving money to her mother and her father. She had a daughter in college and two younger children. The Virgo has two children and a boyfriend who she lived with and to my knowledge, she was not supporting her parents. I would say that a Sagittarius is probably more giving than an Aries.

My brother purchased a classic Cadillac from some older woman who was too elderly to drive. The car sat in the driveway at my mother's house for a year or five. It needed some work, but it was drivable. My brother could have gotten it fixed and drove it, but he was always getting driven around by his friends. In his eyes, he didn't really need a car. He says he bought it because he likes Cadillacs and the price of $800 was hard to pass up. Knowing my brother, he probably bought it because the old woman needed the money.

My brother gave me his car when I returned from Egypt. That was a very generous thing to do. I got it repaired and headed back to North Carolina. My brother does things like this often and not just for me. He is generous with his friends as well. Sagittarius do not hesitate to give their money to help others.

A practical person would see this as a mismanagement of funds, reckless giving, and lack of planning for their own future well-being. If you look at it on a spiritual level, it is selfless. It must be hard for them to live in a world where materialism is more admirable than selflessness.

CAPRICORN

I have a love/hate relationship with Capricorns. They are stubborn. They want to be in charge of your whole life, but they are fun to be around, too. Capricorns talk a lot but not about anything pertaining to a relationship. I find that to be a weird characteristic of theirs. The men talk about all kinds of things but for some reason the relationship he is in, he has no words. Is it because he thinks whatever he says will piss someone off and he doesn't want to argue about it? Or is it because he is trying to hide his feelings? I believe he is hiding his feelings and he doesn't want to argue about it.

I had a conversation with a Capricorn man that I hadn't spoken to in thirty-two years. I

got mad at him in high school. So, as I am talking to him, I say," You took my phone number, but you didn't call." A week had passed.
"People don't call right away. That's not how it works," he said like this was a rule. I'm baffled. We are adults. It works any way we want it to. Then I think about another Capricorn man who waited five years before calling a girl he liked. When he finally went to visit her, she was engaged to be married.

I haven't spoken to the Capricorn since. If I knew that he liked me, I wouldn't have been so quick to dismiss him but I'm an Aries. I'm the type who holds a grudge and I was still bent from the incident in high school. I should have waited before I called him, in hindsight, because Capricorns are sensitive under that stubborn solid exterior. They are not going to tell you that, so no need to ask them.

The Capricorn women I know don't mind arguing or fighting. I saw two different Capricorn women attack their boyfriends. One did it right in front of his parents. The other one threw a cast iron pan at her boyfriend's head. Me? I didn't even understand why the Capricorn women got so angry.

My guess is that Capricorns bottle up how they feel because they don't like to talk about their feelings. I talk about my feelings all day.
"You make me feel sick."
"I feel that you are getting on my nerves."
"I can feel you breathing all my air and I wish you wouldn't."
They talk about everything else accept what is bothering them. They say things like, "Did you hear what happened to Simone?" "What do you think about Nene's dress?" "I didn't like her hair." They like gossip, both the men and the women.

They ignore bad behavior until something makes them explode. Some of them may even tell you but you won't think it's a big deal because that "something" could be something small. It irritates them, and you probably do it all the time. You may be one of those people who repeats themselves and you don't know that when you repeat yourself, it drives them crazy. You might get a frying pan to the head.

It sounds crazy doesn't it. Well, it is but Capricorns like sex, so there's that. If you can figure out that they like attention, you are half way to heaven. Sure, they are negative and a bit lazy. We learn to appreciate Capricorn's stability and their level head. Capricorns are authoritarian and if you trust them, you will let them tell you to sit down and relax because they will tell you that when you need it. They are looking out for your best interests and they care. If you can find one who trusts you and who you can trust, you are a lucky person.

Capricorn people tend to seem really nice. Nicer than Aries. They will jump to help someone, hold doors, carry groceries, and hold babies but not for the people they love. Oh, no. They are nice on the streets but tend to be an asshole at home. Grudges. Yep, they are secretly mad about shit. If you told him you can bring the groceries in by yourself when you were angry with him once, he will remember that. Like Aries, they file petty shit away. Now, you will have to ask the bastard to help you with the groceries. Even then, he may say something like, "oh, now you want my help but in 1994 you told me to kiss your ass and you could carry your own groceries." Petty.

This is the part about them that wears people out. They may say they are joking but we, Aries, know it isn't a joke because we do the same shit. We can be just as petty, but we are different because if we love you enough, we will forget it. If we don't love you enough, we are leaving. Capricorns aren't going anywhere. They will make you suffer for eternity. Can you imagine two people like this living together? The Aries will have to leave him, and it will break the Capricorn's heart. They are stubborn and believe in staying together. If they never get married it's because they didn't find someone they thought would stick it out. They mate for life when or if, they marry.

Capricorns have hobbies that keep them distracted from wanting a relationship if they have been burned in love. They throw themselves into work. Some party but most can be found at home. They are chefs, like Gemini and Pisces.

You may not know this, but Capricorns have fetishes. Don't ask me how I know but they do. They like to do weird stuff in the bedroom like sucking toes, and other kinky things I won't mention. A Capricorn can keep an Aries amused. You're a lucky Aries if you get one of those easy-going and kind natured Capricorns. One of the ones who wants nothing more than to cuddle, eat, have sex, and take care of you.

My only concern with this relationship is that it can become violent. Both personalities are strong, and no one wants to back down. The goat and the ram will butt heads all day. They both sense this about each other and they will do their best not to get into an argument, especially, if they respect each other. Capricorns look up to Aries and Aries admire Capricorns. The difference is that the Capricorn is indifferent to the fights, but the Aries will be shaking to the core. Some Capricorns have an angry temperament. They argue about everything. To some Capricorns, this is just a means to make up sex but to the Aries, it's the beginning of a war that the Capricorn has no idea he's in. You ever hear of a man coming home from work and his wife has packed all of her stuff and is gone? Aries. The Capricorn will not understand why you left. He or she will not understand that even though you don't shy away from combat, you don't want to live in combat on a daily basis. An Aries is more destructive. The way we look at the Leo lose his temper and think, "he's out of control," the Capricorn is looking at us and thinking the same thing. The worst part is our "destruction" will be of the Capricorn's character. We will tell him about himself. We will hurt his feelings. We will tell him all the things we held back for years because we didn't want to argue, and we knew it would ruin him. If the ruination comes, it's because the relationship is OVER.

Capricorns are goats. Just like the ram, the goat uses his head to get dominance. Goats and sheep are related as a species. If you feel like that Capricorn is a bit much to handle, you are seeing yourself in them. Goats are smaller than rams. If you see a crazy animal hanging off the side of a mountain, it's probably a goat. Goats are very social and so are Capricorns. You will find Capricorns at parties, cook outs, and clubs. They don't go as often as Geminis or Libras because they tire easily. They, like the goat, have a period of time where they go solo. They need their alone time.

The key words for Capricorn are I use. A Capricorn must find you useful before he can find a reason to be your friend. This sounds distasteful but it is often the case. Capricorns don't have people who are just hanging around them loafing and enjoying the spoils of their success. It is a tactical way to form friends, but it is how it happens. Capricorns are hard working so most of their friends may be people from work as they spend all their time there. They also have friends who have the same hobbies as them. Which also leads to the usefulness of an individual. I suppose as they get older it is harder for them to make friends. They like to be around people who are doing better than them. People who are successful. I tend to view this as a goat like way to exist, always climbing mountains.

Capricorns are an earth sign and are grounded in their lifestyle. A young Aries will find them boring. Capricorns seem mature even when they are young. As an Aries matures, they realize the stability and maturity of a Capricorn is an asset. Capricorns are cardinal which means they will initiate things. The way I see it with Capricorn is that they always seem to have a lot going on. There is always a project. Things must be mulled over and considered and reconsidered. They want to know what the advantage will be and the benefit. After much consideration, they will start a new endeavor. A Capricorn will have his fingers in many pies and eggs in many baskets.

Capricorns understand that hard works leads to success. They are diligent, patient, and stable. If they are susceptible to advice, they can be great men. If they are hard headed, they will miss opportunities because of their pride. If they are unable to hear and accept what their spouse is saying, they will not be married for long. A good Capricorn is one who is able to compromise. This may be hard for a Capricorn who has been single for a long time. Capricorns can come off as assholes to people. This is because they tend to withdraw when their relationship is not successful, they spend too much time alone, and they become content by themselves. Their tolerance for the foibles of other humans is low. A good Capricorn understands his faults and works on them because his end goal is to be successful in all things. If a Capricorn believes they are more successful single, that is how they will remain. Besides, how useful is a marriage if it will end in divorce? Capricorns want a long-term relationship. If the other person is not marriage material, Capricorns won't stick around long.

AQUARIUS

Aquarius are independent, I can't stress it enough. They don't need you. As for relationships, they don't appear to want those either. All Aquarius like to be free. Some of them get married but they will be free in their marriage. Yes, they will do what they want when they want. Hopefully, you will get a loyal one. If not, expect the same treatment as you would from a Gemini. The worst part of it, you won't know why the Aquarius is distant. At least with the Gemini, you know that they would rather party and have fun. You don't know what the Aquarius is doing. Are they cheating? Maybe. Are they shopping? Maybe. Are they doing drugs? It is possible.

They don't party as much as Gemini, but they like to have fun. Fun to them can be anything though. Clipping their toenails could be fun, cleaning a fish tank, or scrubbing the bathroom floor could be any one of the things they find fun. Their idea of fun doesn't always meet the traditional description.

Aries get along with Aquarius because our quirks don't bother them. They don't seem to have any complaints but when they do have complaints you will hear about them. They do not hold their tongue. They are not mean or malicious and they don't try to hurt your feelings. They don't hold grudges.

Most of the Aquarius I know are positive people and they will defend their friends and family. People don't talk about this a lot, but Aquarius people do not back down. I have seen them defend themselves without fighting. When something is wrong it is wrong and there is no convincing an Aquarius otherwise. But they will fight, if pushed.

Aquarius want to be their parent's favorite child. They go out of their way to take care of their parents until they are satisfied that they have achieved their goal. If their parents don't need to be taken care of the Aquarius will be sure to visit and call often. It goes along with their need to get attention. Most of the time the Aquarius is the youngest, but it doesn't matter where they fall in the group of siblings

Aquarius make good friends. They are the kind of friend that you don't see for a while but it's like they never disappeared when they return. There is no holding an Aquarius down because they have things to do, by themselves. Getting angry about it won't do any good because it will happen again. They have a lot of friends and will hang out with each one, one on one. They rarely blend their friends. I don't know any Aquarius that have thrown a party but they like going to parties. Geminis, Capricorns, Virgos, Leos, and Libras throw parties often. Aries, Taurus, and Aquarius like to help with the food and decorations. Of course, Aries is in charge of the food and decorations. Even if no one said we are, we naturally become the one people are asking for advice. Should I put the food here? What should I bring? Does this centerpiece look good? It never fails.

The keywords for the Aquarius are I know. I don't want to say Aquarius's are know it all's but, they are. They think they know why you exist. They think they know why you are suffering. Don't believe me? Ask them. I have a relative who tells me often, I know why you are going through what you are going through. I never ask her what she thinks she knows. Who knows? She may be right. Aquarius people observe and analyze everything but the difference between them and the Virgo is that the Aquarius does not take themselves seriously. Everything is easy with them. They are not offended if you don't ask. Often, the Aquarius will keep the answer to themselves.

Aquarius are water bearers which literally means they carry water. Water is very important to life. It is the beginning and ending of everything. Water holds a lot of weight in the existence of all things living and breathing. Without it, we die. Now, that

I think of it, I may start asking my Aquarius relative what she knows. Every existential crisis I go through, she says, "I know why you are suffering." I may need to consult with my relative.

Aquarius people are Air signs which means they like to move about. They like their freedom. They are a fixed sign which means they are who they are and will rarely change on you. You will know who they are because they don't hide their faults or eccentricities. Aquarius people are odd that way. They don't care if you know who they are as a person. They are authentic. Most people don't want you to see their bad side or their emotional side. Not the Aquarius. They don't care what you think about them. They tend to be cheerful and happy people. They don't do a lot of complaining. They like a lot of attention but then, they disappear. No hard feelings, they need to do whatever crazy thing they like to do. They'll be back.

Aquarius people are talkative, and they like to share information. I wouldn't say they are gossips but they can be. They are opinionated but not offensive. They only time I have met an Aquarius that I didn't like was one who was under pressure. She was argumentative, disagreeable, and scattered brained. I found out that her father was ill, and she was also having some medical issues.

People act differently when things are going wrong in their lives. You can't judge a person from their behavior alone. Sometimes, you have to look deeper at how someone handles adversity. Life isn't always going to go smoothly or in your favor. As an Aries, I retreat. I don't want to hang out or talk. I am not going to burden anyone with my issues. You will never know that I have any serious issues. I mind my business and carry on. Being angry and mistreating others is not going to solve anyone's problems. You will only make enemies out of people who may have been helpful.

PISCES

My Pisces friends are good friends. They like to take us with them when they need protection. We are good friends to them because they can be themselves no matter how weird. They are weird. They live in their own world and Aries don't care.

Pisces are hard to understand because they keep to themselves. They keep a lot inside.

They are emotional. They keep a lot of emotion under wraps, but their emotions will break free from time to time. You won't catch a Pisces crying. They cry privately. You will catch them losing their temper. They can hold a grudge for a long time. Yet, Pisces are very helpful and friendly.

Pisces are not very professional, or business minded but they are not stupid. The reason they are not business minded (unless their chart has other signs in the rising and moon) is because they spend a lot of time in a fantasy world. Their fantasy life crosses into their real life. It's not so much fantasy but living in a different dimension. It isn't a fantasy as much as it is a different world. The pain they live with is easier to cope with if they create another world to live in.

I worked with two Pisces women. They worked completely based on enthusiasm. They didn't have any experience. They didn't exactly learn quickly either, but people liked them and trusted their presumed ability. They made mistakes and wanted to create a work environment that wasn't based on practical business practices. It was frustrating to me. I like to work in a standard work environment where proven methods worked, and skill mattered. I like process, organization, and structure. I would often catch both women staring into the abyss. When they both got promoted, I knew I was working at the wrong place.

Unlike Scorpio, Pisces doesn't have to get high or drunk to live in this world. They are naturally drawn to the other world. If Pisces drinks or gets high, it's to live in the real world. If the Scorpio drinks and gets high, it's to go to another world. Pisces doesn't have deep thoughts, they are just deep. It flows out of them. They are people who live at the bottom of the ocean, but their body is physically here on earth.

For example, I was sitting with a little five-year-old Pisces girl who had met me before. This was her second time meeting me. I was dating her uncle. She said, "You seem different."
I thought it was odd to say but I remembered that she is a Pisces. Instead of brushing the comment off, I asked her what she meant. Any other kid would just be observing my outward appearance whereas a Pisces would have a more intrusive observation. She said, "Your heart is beating faster." Weird right?

So, I thought about it. When she met me the first time, I hugged her. I was driving with her uncle. We drove a long distance, and I was exhausted but calm. We took a nap the minute we arrived at her house. This time when she met me and I hugged her, we were at a family reunion around a lot of people and although I looked calm, I wasn't. Pisces. What type of demon child notices that?

This is the thing about Pisces that will get on your nerves; Pisces like to dissect everything you say trying to find the hidden meaning or to let you know how "smart" or "clever" they are. For example, I said, "Reading comprehension is a skill." Pisces said, "I don't understand. What do you mean? Is this in reference to something? What does comprehension mean?" Funny right? Not to me. I'm looking at this adult like, you know exactly what I mean, and I don't intend to give you the definition of comprehension. A Pisces will challenge every single word you say to make a sarcastic joke. Which is okay if you are speaking to each other one on one. But no. The Pisces will do this in front of the class and will frustrate the poor teacher. He is trying to make her look like a fool. If she is an Aries and has little patience, he will be headed to the principal's office for disrupting the class.

My brother is Pisces. He has been an odd bird his whole life. The older he gets-the weirder. He notices things and says things based on the tone of your voice. Other people are too busy breathing. When our father died, I wanted to view the body at the morgue. I am not bothered by dead bodies at all. If I am, I won't let on. We are riding around for hours running errands for the funeral. I did not mention the morgue all day. Finally, my brother says, "Turn here."
I'm like, "Where are we going?"
"To the morgue."
"I thought you forgot."
He said, "I knew you really wanted to go when you said it the first time." I did and I only said it once. With everything going on, he kept a mental note of that.

Other weird shenanigans with Pisces, they care but will not say. If they do say it, it will be said in a weird way. They have a funny sense of humor. Pisces seem old when they are young. They don't necessarily look old, they act old. Life seems very hard to a Pisces and it usually is very hard on them. They internalize everything.

The Pisces keywords are I believe. The Pisces has a deep belief system. It's complicated. They are very in tune with a higher power without doing anything. I am fascinated by them, but I couldn't date one. I think the Pisces/Aries relationship works better when the man is an Aries and the woman is a Pisces, but he should be careful not to bruise her emotionally. Otherwise, we are better as friends. Aries learn from Pisces by observing and vice versa. This relationship is more of a spiritual trade. What I have, they want, and what they have, I need. I am not talking about materials things. I am referring to spiritual connections. The bad part of this is how serious Pisces can be with their spiritual connection and it puts some people off them. Pisces spend a lot of time hiding who they are. If anyone is wearing a mask, it's a Pisces. Not because they want to hide, it's because they know people will not understand them. They would be ostracized. Everyone walks around talking about how they love Jesus but if Jesus was walking about speaking the way he speaks and working miracles, people would be afraid of him.

Pisces are mutable which means they are capable of change. They can accept change better than most. As a water sign, they are most like water. Fish represent Pisces and that says a lot about them. Fish can hide in the deep. They can go far below the surface and you would never see them. Who knows what fish are doing? Who knows what fish are thinking? It's the same for Pisces. Fish have a secret world under the ocean.

I've never known a Pisces to pick a friend based on the clothes they wear or popularity. Pisces select people because they like them. Who do they like? I never know why Pisces pick their friends. They seem like a rag tag group of people. Pisces are somewhat similar to Leos who like the underdog. Pisces like the sad. Sad people from every corner. They get angry and stop talking to you. They will tell you how shitty you are and then after a few months, they will slowly come around. Pisces are very controlling. They want to control their friends lives. They want to be in charge of where you go and what you do.

Pisces are stalkerish. They want to know what you are doing and where you are going. Scorpios will watch you. Cancers will ask you. Pisces will follow you. Water signs want to know everything about you. It's intrusive.

Made in the USA
Monee, IL
29 May 2021